CASSELL STUDIES IN PASTORAL CARE AND PERSONAL AND SOCIAL EDUCATION

D0195202

DEATH AND LOSS

CASSELL STUDIES IN PASTORAL CARE AND PERSONAL
AND SOCIAL EDUCATION

DEATH AND LOSS

*Compassionate Approaches in
the Classroom*

Oliver Leaman

NATIONAL UNIVERSITY
LIBRARY   SAN DIEGO

CASSELL

Cassell
Wellington House   387 Park Avenue South
125 Strand   New York
London WC2R 0BB   NY 10016–8810

© Oliver Leaman 1995

All rights reserved. No part of this publication may be reproduced or
transmitted in any form or by any means, electronic or mechanical including
photocopying, recording or any information storage or retrieval system,
without prior permission in writing from the publishers.

British Library Cataloguing-in-Publication Data
A catalogue record for this book is available from the British Library.

ISBN 0–304–33087–6 (hardback)
    0–304–33089–2 (paperback)

Phototypeset by Intype, London
Printed and bound in Great Britain by Biddles Limited, Guildford and
King's Lynn

Contents

Series editors' foreword

Many schools and individual teachers are aware of society's ambivalent and unsatisfactory attitudes to death. For many it is, after all, still the 'last taboo'. They also recognize that children and young people are concerned about and interested in the area, yet it remains the case that the amount of work done in schools which is devoted to death is very limited. Where work is done, it is often reactive, 'after the event', and handled uneasily, or, in the case of a major tragedy, left to experts brought in from outside. In such circumstances, any book which assists schools in their work with pupils and develops the support they are able to offer must be welcome.

However, what Oliver Leaman has written is not just a handbook but something more profound. Not everyone will agree with all that he says – indeed, many of his arguments are controversial – but those who read the book will be forced to think in new and radical ways about this important and neglected issue. Moreover, his ideas should encourage reflection about issues within a much wider area of schools' work, including much that is encompassed by Pastoral Care and Personal and Social Education and the relationships these should involve. In particular, the more general themes of loss and risk are considered not only in their relation to death, but in themselves as highly significant human experiences and motivations.

A great strength of this book is that Oliver Leaman's theoretical ideas and practical suggestions have both been developed from recent and relevant evidence. Although not a research report in the conventional sense, this evidence is the result of extensive research which collected data from pupils, teachers and others. Some of the data relate to pupils or teachers who have recently experienced the effects of a major tragedy as well as those who have confronted death at an individual level.

Oliver Leaman argues that attitudes to death are best understood when coupled with the closely related concepts of loss and risk. He believes that these are some of the most central concerns for human beings, ones that are held in common by us all. The implication of this is that schools should include some consideration of them in the curriculum. However, the theoretical perspective which he has developed means that such work will need to be quite radically conceived in terms of both approach and relationship.

The key arguments which distinguish this book from others dealing with this area are twofold: first, that typically members of the working class have attitudes to death, loss and risk which are different from those of the middle classes; second, that in cases of bereavement what is helpful and appropriate for one individual may not be so for another. Schools will need to take both these facts to heart in their attempts to help children cope in such circumstances.

Oliver Leaman's work suggests that some schools are far better able to handle tragedy and the needs that this creates in both pupils and teachers because of the more open relationships which exist within their organization. It is clear that these more 'open' schools provide examples of good practice which go well beyond their handling of death and tragedy. At the heart of his argument is the centrality to human experience of death, loss and risk, and the view that these should, therefore, be part of the curriculum. Further, as there are no 'experts' in this area – both teachers and pupils approach death as a great unknown – the work implies a new, more open and productive relationship between teachers and pupils.

Schools and individual teachers will find this both a fascinating and a useful book, a book that has implications for their attitudes, understanding and practice. We believe it makes an unusual and valuable addition to our series.

Peter Lang
Ron Best

Preface

I first thought of writing this book when I was sitting in a classroom in Bootle shortly after the disaster at Hillsborough. A large number of Liverpool Football Club supporters had been killed or injured during the chaos before the game against Sheffield Wednesday. Many of the casualties were young people, and hardly a school in Merseyside avoided having a pupil involved, or so it seemed when one visited schools. I was watching a teacher talking about the tragedy, and it became clear to me that he had no idea what to say, and that the pupils were seeking a lead from him which he was unable to provide. Later on in the day I left that secondary school and went to an infant school in the same area. There was a child in the class who had just experienced the sudden death of her father at home, and the school members were in turmoil as to how they should behave towards her. The teachers were worried because she did not display any apparent grieving behaviour and answered the questions of her friends about the death in entirely pragmatic ways. The teachers thought that this would lead to a great deal of psychological trouble later, and had no idea what they should say to her, or to the other children in the class. It struck me then as remarkable that this common feature of humanity, the fact that we will all eventually die, is entirely ignored by schools. Teachers have no idea what they should say about death and dying, and take energetic steps to avoid the issue.

I decided to visit a large variety of schools around the country and examine the strategies they employ in dealing with death. I expected, for example, that the attitude of denominational schools would differ from that of secular schools. This book has grown out of those visits and shows how a wide variety of schools in England, particularly in urban communities, handle death. It occurred to me during the research that death as a concept is strongly linked to notions such as loss and risk, and that these should also be examined. I never expected a set of guidelines to emerge as to how these ideas should be explored with children, and readers will not find such a blueprint here. I propose that teachers and pupils should work out their own solutions, and I discuss some possible approaches. I also point out ways in which death may be introduced into the curriculum and into the structure of schooling in general, and I put forward some reasons for doing so.

My main debt is to the large number of pupils and teachers who were prepared to talk to me about these issues. Sometimes they found it upsetting to do so, and I am very grateful to them for sharing their feelings and ideas with me. Although these conversations were often depressing, with the interviewer and the children sometimes close to, or actually in, tears, there was laughter too, and a general feeling by my respondents that this was an important topic about which a lot more needs to be known. All the names have been changed, and no details of either respondents or schools have been provided here which could identify them.

I should like to thank the National Children's Bureau for electing me to a Kellmer Pringle Fellowship, which enabled me to carry out the research. The views expressed in this book are in no way to be identified with the views of the National Children's Bureau. I have presented some of my findings at conferences in Oxford, Eastbourne and Chicago, and I should like to thank the participants for their comments. Those of us who are interested in working in the area of children and death are used to getting rather strange looks from people who obviously think that this is a peculiar topic to investigate. I am grateful to all those who gave me the benefit of the doubt and who were prepared to talk to me. I hope that they will feel that this final product justifies their involvement.

Oliver Leaman
Liverpool, June 1994

Introduction

The structure of this book is quite simple. It starts off by looking at society's attitudes to death and then examines the attitudes prevalent in different sorts of school. It will be seen that different social and occupational groups have different attitudes to death, and that teachers are especially anxious about the place of death in the curriculum. Although many people would argue that death is an inappropriate topic for children, there is a good deal of evidence that children are very curious about death and would benefit from its introduction into schooling. Children obviously differ in their attitudes towards death, and age plays a part in this, but the individual child's experience of loss through death might be made use of as a teaching and learning resource. Moreover, teachers should be encouraged to tackle their own anxieties about death before they can usefully discuss it with their pupils.

Talking to children about death is not straightforward and teachers should be aware of the pitfalls. It is easy to upset children and reopen emotional wounds which have taken a long time to heal. Talking about death is not an esoteric extra to be added on to the curriculum: it should be part of the activity of encouraging children to work out their own feelings in response to situations involving loss or risk. Those notions already fall within the range of teacher-pupil discussion, since teachers encourage their pupils to adopt a mature attitude to their lives and draw attention to the risks involved in participating in dangerous activities. The notion of risk is not objective, though, and it is difficult to give a definition of an acceptable risk which will satisfy both teachers and pupils. By getting children to think about death it is possible to ensure that they have genuinely considered the potential consequences of their actions, and it can enable teachers and pupils to participate in a genuine dialogue in which both parties exchange views which are treated with equal respect.

It is important to distinguish between disasters and ordinary tragedies, the latter being deaths which have a primarily private focus. Public disasters are in some ways easier to bear, since they are subject to a great deal of attention, and they may lead to the arrival of professional help for the bereaved. Private deaths are far harder to come to terms with, and teachers should be aware of the ways in which these can interfere with the educational progress of pupils. Teachers are often important players in the emotional lives of their pupils, and they cannot ignore the role they should play in helping those pupils. There are dangers in relying on counsellors to help children over such problems, since there is evidence that children may feel manipulated by counsellors who insist that they respond to death in a particular manner. It is also dangerous for teachers to rely on conventional or ready-made tactics when trying to cope with bereaved children, and adults in general should respect the personal nature of each child's grief.

The notion of death may be present throughout the curriculum, or only in a specific subject area. I am in favour of the former, since it is a more effective teaching strategy to approach a difficult concept such as death through the curriculum as a whole. There is also a role for teachers with specific expertise to help pupils who are having problems with bereavement, yet we should not assume that talking about death should be limited to those teachers. They may not have a sufficiently developed relationship with the pupils concerned to be useful in this respect. The topics of death, risk and loss should be recurrent in all teacher-pupil interaction, since only then will it be possible to discuss them in an effective manner. Schools in which these and other problematic topics can be raised serve as more successful communities than schools where this is not possible.

There has been little research concerning methods of talking to schoolchildren about death. The review of published works at the end of this book is little more than a list of what is available, with occasional comments. There is an excellent choice of books for all ages and levels of ability dealing with death and bereavement, but it would be invidious to point to particular books as being especially useful, since different children and teachers will find different books appropriate to their needs. There is no shortage of material for the construction of courses. In fact, children are far better served than adults. They have a choice among some excellent books, while adults have to rely on works which tend to present death from the point of view of popular psychology, philosophy or history, the sorts of books which offer platitudes in the guise of significant insights designed to make the reader feel better about herself. Although much of the academic research assumes that death is a social taboo, there are many books on the topic in bookshops – it is disappointing, however, how few of them go into any depth. The thesis of this book is that death is far too important a topic to be left to the popularizers who write about 'relationships' and who try to make us feel good about ourselves and our lives. That is why the subject of death should be integrated into the school curriculum. It is a subject which naturally interests children, and teachers have a responsibility to respond to this interest by talking to children about death. We shall see what are the problems and possibilities of doing so.

What is being presented here is by no means a comprehensive report on the topic of death, loss and risk, and their educational implications.

This is a vast area in which much work has already been carried out, and which requires far more research than has so far been accomplished. The research which the author carried out has a wider scope than can be defined here. What has been attempted is to illustrate some of the key issues in the area of research, together with some possible strategies for helping teachers and pupils work together in schools when discussing death, loss and risk. The section on methodology outlines some of the ways of investigating these issues, but it is not suggested that only one methodological perspective on the issue is acceptable. On the contrary, it would be helpful to have a wide variety of theoretical perspectives, and these do exist in the literature, as the 'Guide to the Literature' shows; references are provided to texts which discuss the topic within an experimental context not shared by the work described here. Again, there is no attempt to be comprehensive, but just to give an indication of how rich and varied the debate has been, by listing texts which readers might find interesting and challenging.

A free man thinks of nothing less than of death, and his wisdom is a meditation on life, not on death.

Spinoza, *Ethics* IV, Proposition 67

CHAPTER 1

The attitude of schools to death

One would expect the attitude of schools to death to be closely related to the attitude of society. Schools are in many ways a microcosm of society and therefore accurate reflectors of social attitudes and trends. Much of the research into the relationship between schooling and society has emphasized the role of schools as a force for socialization. It follows from this that the key messages which society seeks to relay are likely to be found in schools. The role of schools in preparing children for adult life in society involves the transmission of established modes of thinking. This is not to say that education is a simple passing on of accepted social values to children through the school system. The link between schools and society is far more complex than any picture of schools just reflecting society and reproducing it through the educational process would suggest. Schools differ widely, and pupils and teachers vary in their ability to resist indoctrination in current ideology. Schools may also present a view of society which is inaccurate or more extreme than reality, and the content of education cannot be reduced to a check-list of social values. We should beware of any explanation of the link between school and society which seeks to simplify what must be a highly diverse and complicated relationship.

While schools are not just a reflection of society, they are clearly going to be heavily influenced by the society in which they are situated. But society is not the only factor which influences schools. The families from which the children come also have a very important impact upon the nature of schooling, and the ideas that children bring with them to school from home may be realistically expected to have a significant impact upon the way in which schools work. This becomes very clear when the teachers are from different class or ethnic backgrounds from their pupils. Teachers may discover that they have very different values and ambitions from their pupils, and they may pause to consider the difficulties of trying to impose an alien system of ideas upon those pupils. Middle-class teachers in working-class areas often compare themselves with missionaries in the jungle, surrounded by deprived and woefully mis-guided savages who must be instructed with the right attitudes and knowledge if they are to be saved from their environment! A good deal of research suggests that schooling is likely to be most effective where the messages which children receive at home are in line with those transmitted at school, so that education and upbringing reinforce each other. What *is* clear is the importance of the influence which family and home have on the pupil, and any effective teacher has to take this into account before designing lessons, or, indeed, a whole curriculum.

It is important to explore the ideas about death which are current in society at large before looking at how those ideas are developed in schools. This establishes the context within which schools function, and until we understand that context we cannot hope to grasp the possibilities and difficulties which attend the concept of death in education. Yet it must be borne in mind that it is impossible to generalize about such an important concept as death. Different communities in this country have very different attitudes towards death, and, as we shall see, different occupational groups also differ in attitude. The media present a wide range of views, and different religions each have their own teaching. Were one to stop a random number of individuals in the street and ask them for their attitudes to death, one might expect to hear many different and distinct points of view. For example, one respondent might say that she never thought about death and that it played no part in her attitude towards the activities of her life. Someone else might say that he spent a lot of time thinking about it, and that he constantly wondered about the purpose of human action given the ubiquity of death. Another individual might answer in line with adherence to a particular religious or personal faith, and present the views of that tradition, perhaps with some personal embellishments. Despite this diversity, it is possible to make some general remarks about the ways in which the phenomenon of death is perceived in our society, and to connect those perceptions with proposals for dealing with the topic of death in schools.

One of the contrasts which is immediately apparent between contemporary society and that of our Victorian predecessors lies in the customs and behaviour surrounding death. In the past, far more fuss was made over funerals, bereavement and grief than would be usual today. It would be wrong to conclude from this that we actually suffer less today than our Victorian ancestors when people who are close to us die, but it is worth reflecting on this change in social customs. People today are often more self-conscious when grieving, as though they were unsure what the appropriate conduct should be. There is indeed today little or no received etiquette to prescribe appropriate behaviour in a given situation, and this includes bereavement. One reason for this is our comparative unfamiliarity with this area of human experience. Life expectancy is higher today than a hundred years ago, and families are smaller. Good nutrition and health are taken for granted, and we have fewer close family ties than in the past. It is also perhaps the case that we have fewer close relationships altogether, within or outside the family, than our ancestors. Most people in this country live in urban communities and may be expected to be mobile in search of work and housing, with the consequence that fewer friendships may be initiated and social life may have become more fragmented. One's circle of acquaintances and the number of people for whom one cares may become reduced. As more traditional communities are broken up and reconstituted in different forms in different places, the individual is less able to sustain long-lasting relationships. This is not an inevitable aspect of urban life, but there does seem to be a trend in modern political and economic changes to emphasize the individual and reduce the importance of communal life. In the modern world more people are self-employed, work part-time or work in smaller units than in the past, and this necessarily hampers the formation and durability of the sorts of social network which existed in the past. One feature of this is that the individual may come to see others as competitors for work rather than as potential friends, and there may be fewer people in the workforce with whom to initiate relationships of friendship or solidarity. Urban redevelopment has led to the decline of well-established working-class communities which supported a rich network of social and political relationships.

These changes to the social fabric and their implications for politics, crime and health have been well-documented and much discussed, but they also affect our perceptions of death. With smaller families, and fewer ties of affection and respect, coupled with longer life expectancy, the average person will suffer fewer losses from death than his counterpart several generations ago. Death will be relatively unfamiliar, and there will perhaps be a tendency to feel unsure about how to act in the face of it. Nowadays death usually takes place in hospital and is distanced from the patient's family by hospital routine and medical technology. The dead body is normally collected from the hospital by the undertakers and retained by them until burial or cremation. The body will be disposed of in a relatively swift manner, with little ceremony, and the bereaved friends and relations will be expected to get back to normal life quickly. Although many disposals will involve a religious service, it is unlikely that many of the participants will have strong religious beliefs, since there has been a rapid decline in religious affiliation in this century. This is very different from the practices of the past, when many people died at home in the company of their family, the body being then prepared by the family or undertakers to lie in the home before the funeral, so that mourners could view the body until the ceremony itself. Very elaborate clothes and rituals would often be involved, and the bereaved would be expected to display quite dramatic grief behaviour at the funeral itself, and to keep up a vestige of that behaviour for some considerable period afterwards. The character of the funeral itself was likely to be strongly religious and the participants would be expected to be adherents of some faith. Since families were larger and life expectancy shorter, one might expect to attend quite a few of these ceremonies during one's life. Of course, the expenditure incurred was dependent upon the financial standing of the people concerned, but there is no doubt that a relatively high proportion of income was devoted to paying for undertakers and the ritual surrounding funerals. For many people it was necessary to insure against such a major expense, which they otherwise could not have afforded.

Industrial societies have changed a lot in the last hundred years or so. Whereas in the past the economies of such societies were based on production, today they are based on consumption. Consumption has become a vital aspect of how we relate to each other and to society at large, and those who for one reason or another do not have the means to consume are highly marginal individuals. They may feel entitled to own things which everyone else owns even when they do not have the means to buy them. Status is very much dependent upon the ability to consume, and one of the apparently absurd features of death in our society is that it brings about an end to consumption. This has led to the development of societies which tend to deny the existence of death, ignoring it when it occurs and taking highly elaborate steps to avoid it or put it off for as long as possible. When we look at the attitude of different occupational and social groups to death we shall see how this affects particular types of individual, but it can be said of society as a whole that it reacts very negatively to the phenomenon of death. Death has replaced sex as the final taboo. While people in contemporary society are prepared to be relatively open about sex, death remains a little-discussed issue, one which we are happier to leave in a medical context and ignore in so far as we can. Although we frequently see death in a stylized form on the television, we observe real death very rarely. It is sanitized and medicalized out of our presence as far as it can be, and we do all that we can to remove it physically from us.

What implications does this have for schools? One might think that schools have to limit the number of topics and issues which they can consider as part of the curriculum, and that death is not a subject which should concern young people. After all, if society at large tends to ignore death, and if it is in accordance with the customs of the time to avoid this topic, then perhaps schools should just follow suit. This is a mis-guided, albeit common, strategy. Death does enter the school, often in ways of which the school is largely unaware. Many children will know people who have died or who are dying, and they may have difficulties in confronting these facts. These difficulties are amplified by the ways in which death is ignored in society, so that such children may feel that they are utterly alone in having to deal with their feelings. Much of the curriculum, however, does relate quite directly to death. This involves those aspects of the curriculum which deal with risk, with health and with the life-styles of children and adults. In that teachers spend a lot of time telling children how they should behave, and what steps they should take to preserve the length and quality of their lives, they are indirectly touching on attitudes to death. It seems to me that one of the reasons why this part of the curriculum is so unsuccessful at the moment is that the direct connection with death is not made by either teachers or their pupils, and without this direct connection it is unlikely that the curriculum will be effective. In such encounters the teachers and pupils have a poor understanding of each other's habits of thought, and the result is often a clash of attitudes rather than a genuine interchange of views, leading to conflict rather than mutual understanding. As death is already present in school culture, ignoring its role in the activities of the school is to ignore its role in the experiences of the children and to devalue the effectiveness of the curriculum.

This might seem to be a rather sweeping observation. Few children will be expected to have serious psychological problems connected with bereavement, and many have had no experiences which have brought them close to death. Very few young people die in our society any more, and since families are now quite small, with grandparents perhaps living elsewhere, it is unlikely that many young people will have had anything to do directly with the death of close friends or relatives. Television exposes children to death, both fictional and real, and this familiarity could breed indifference, leaving the child unprepared for bereavement in her own life. It is nonetheless not uncommon for young people to have come into contact with real deaths of people close to them, and to encounter difficulties in dealing with those experiences. It is important here to consider the importance of class on death statistics. In general people are healthier than in the past and longer-lived, and this is to some extent a reflection of improved living standards. People from mainly working-class communities have a lower life expectancy than those from more prosperous social groups, and males are likely to die at a younger age than females. The life-styles of people in poorer communities are less conducive to health and long life than those enjoyed in higher-income communities. Children may be obliged to play in the streets, and the more macho culture which predominates at a lower social level may encourage boys in particular to do so. Their parents may be more likely to smoke, with an effect upon the behaviour of their children, and they may eat less wholesome food. Since adults in deprived communities lack power, they tend to have higher rates of heart and mental disease than their more prosperous peers, so children are likely to have a heightened awareness of both medical problems and death if they grow up in such communities.

We can usefully contrast the life-style of such children with that of their teachers. The latter are likely to be middle-class, or at least to have middle-class aspirations, and may also be middle-aged. Most of them will be risk-averse, with pension plans, mortgages and quite possibly families. They may be concerned about their health, about what they eat and the environment in which they live, and they may take steps to follow a prudent regimen. They may be very enthusiastic about communicating to their pupils their views on how one ought to live carefully, while the pupils may seem to have quite opposite and imprudent ideas about how to behave. Teachers are often eager to recommend their interests to their pupils, whether in sport, literature, television or whatever, since they commonly regard their lives as more organized than those of their pupils, and see their role partly as making pupils aware of alternative courses of action and life-style. One element of the education process is to make pupils aware of a wider range of ideas and ways of living than those with which they were previously acquainted, thereby presenting them with alternatives when they thought that there was only one way of doing things. It is always difficult, when engaged in such instruction, to avoid being patronizing, since many teachers feel that their way of life is in fact superior to that of their pupils. They feel that if their pupils were able to grasp what was being offered to them, and accepted the necessity for change, they would be acting in their own best interests.

One of the things which teachers notice about their pupils is that they may have a rather casual attitude to their own safety. For example, if a lesson is being given on AIDS and on the necessity to take precautions to avoid infection, many children appear to be quite apathetic about their own safety. It is interesting that many AIDS educators report that children take much the same attitude towards AIDS as they take, and as their pre-AIDS predecessors took, to unwanted pregnancy. This is not to suggest that such education is not effective, for it clearly is for some children. But for those children who are prepared to take risks, who live in an environment in which risk-taking is a regular and respectable activity, the fact that they find it difficult to distinguish between the risk of AIDS and the risk of pregnancy (and sexually transmitted diseases) is significant. AIDS educators often emphasize the difference between these two possible consequences of unprotected sexual contact, and discuss in detail the necessity to consider forms of contraception which protect against both, as though their audience finds it difficult to understand the distinction. What the teachers themselves fail to understand here is that many children are prepared to accept high levels of risk as reasonable, and would not be critical of their friends and partners who do the same. In many ways, risk is a social category, and it is because teachers do not often understand this that their lessons lack effectiveness. Those lessons seem from the point of view of the teachers to be about prolonging and enhancing the quality of life. From the point of view of at least some of the children they are about trying to impose on them a way of behaving which is contrary to their desires and interests.

We have yet again to return to the concept of death. What teachers are saying when they warn schoolchildren about particular practices like smoking, unprotected sex, joy-riding, glue-sniffing, drug abuse and so on is not just that these activities are bad for one, but that they are potentially lethal. They can end not only in the death of the participants, but also in the deaths of others run over or infected by the participants. Yet children are not invited to think about those deaths, nor about their own death, since we do not as a society find it easy or even acceptable to think about such a topic. Yet the topic of death is there in the background, and the more one attempts to ignore it the more firmly it makes its presence felt. Teachers imply through their work in these areas of the curriculum that we should put a high value on life, and on a particular way of living, and that this involves taking appropriate steps to ensure that life continues for as long as possible. Pupils may agree that life has a high value and is to be preserved at all costs, but their idea of 'life' may be very different from their teachers'. They may feel that an acceptable life-style should involve some degree of risk which could result in a shorter, albeit more exciting, lifespan.

One might well expect younger people to have a different attitude to risk from older people. It does not require much research to establish the truth of this generalization. Younger people normally feel healthier, stronger and more confident of their place in the scheme of things than older people who may well have already experienced illness, bereavement and a series of emotional or professional disappointments which have made them more cautious in their behaviour. The insurance companies recognize this fact in charging lower premiums for older drivers and house-owners. Of course, this is a generalization, and no doubt there are plenty of reckless elderly drivers and cautious young drivers, yet it would be difficult to argue that the old are likely to be more imprudent than the young. So much of our experience goes against it.

Significant differences in attitudes to risk could be due to class. Middle-class occupations tend to be healthier than working-class occupations, and middle-class people may put a higher premium on health and life than do working-class people. In some ways this is paradoxical, since few middle-class occupations occasion bouts of ill-health, or even quite considerable disablement. Such work is often based upon mental effort and can continue even in quite difficult physical conditions from the point of view of the agent. Yet many working-class occupations depend upon strength and high levels of health, and once this is jeopardized, it is impossible to carry on working. One might expect, then, that working-class people would be more concerned about their health than members of the middle class, but this does not appear to be the case.

Why not? It is not difficult to think of good reasons for this difference. To acquire middle-class work, a fairly lengthy process of accreditation and training is often involved. Examinations must be passed, courses completed, and this requires the cultivation of long-term goals. If one considers the process of taking a degree it is obvious that the candidate has to spend a number of years doing things which she may not particularly enjoy, things which are often boring and unfulfilling and which appear to have no purpose in themselves. The student may have to live in a part of the country which is far from family and friends, and it may cost a lot of money to support herself while pursuing her studies. A good deal of mental effort may also be necessary, and the student might find this hard and unfamiliar, especially as it is accompanied by an extended period of relative poverty. When one considers the structure of the traditional career path, aspects of the training process arise yet again. The worker, in seeking to rise through the organization, will have to identify those whom it is useful to cultivate, what sorts of positions she should seek to occupy in the organization, what further training might be required, and so on. A moderately ambitious person will have to consider each move in terms of her career aims, and the way she will seek recognition for her efforts.

Let us contrast this with a working-class person's job prospects. The work may well require a process of training, but it is likely to be shorter and more closely related to the eventual employment. That is to say, the trainee will receive a training which bears a direct resemblance to what the training is for, and so he will be in no doubt as to the point of what he is doing. Once the worker is trained he may have job mobility but it is unlikely to be vertical. He is unlikely to move out of a fairly narrow category of work to doing a different sort of job within an organization. As he ages, he becomes less valuable as an employee, because his physical skills may be an important part of what he does. For the employee to become a higher-paid and more valued part of the organization he would have to acquire the skills and qualifications which would enable him to compete with people from middle-class backgrounds, and this would necessitate a change of perspective, for example being prepared to put up with a lot of difficulties now in order to gain advantages later, something most people in working-class occupations will not see as possible or even desirable for them. They may well have been brought up by their parents and schools to slot into certain sorts of work and are not able culturally to see themselves doing something radically different.

Again, we are dealing with huge generalizations here, and doubtless many counter-examples could be produced. There is also evidence of a major change in working patterns, leading to a general deskilling of both working- and middle-class occupations, and a decrease in any prospect of a job for life. There is undoubtedly also a blurring of the differences between the classes in a society which is increasingly becoming more prosperous and technological, and where people dress and enjoy themselves in increasingly similar ways. Yet it is still true that class has a major influence upon the individual's attitude to life, and therefore also to death. Many working-class respondents have a much clearer notion of death than do their middle-class peers, and this may be expected to influence the attitudes of children in school. Although most people in our society can realistically expect death to occur at the end of a relatively long life, working-class children may have greater awareness of the vagaries of life in that a greater number of their acquaintances are likely to have come to an untimely end. This leads to a greater acceptance of what is seen as chance, and a sharper awareness of the omnipresence of death. Most importantly, it leads to a higher level of risk being accepted, a level of risk which is higher than would be acceptable to middle-class children.

This is very difficult for teachers to understand. They wish to point out to their pupils the dangers of various kinds of activities, and they find that they are regarded as peddling an inappropriate attitude to death. Just as teachers suggest that their pupils read certain books and watch particular television programmes, they also advocate a certain attitude to risk which is foreign to the way in which many of their pupils have been brought up. Teachers are just as unlikely to be successful in converting their pupils to their view of risk as they are in persuading them to change their television-viewing behaviour, or to join the local library. This is not to suggest that teachers in such situations have no effect upon pupils. Of course, they often do. But it is worth being aware of the potential difficulties here. The teachers are trying to make their pupils think like themselves, and this certainly involves agreement across an age barrier and quite possibly across a class barrier as well. What often develops is a clash of views whereby neither side really understands the position of the other. What the teachers cannot understand is why the children appear to be quite reckless in their attachment to behaviour which the teachers perceive as risky. What the pupils cannot understand is why the teachers appear to be so much in favour of a life-style which is so foreign to the children themselves. The more stubborn the pupils are, the more teachers may press them, and the more the pupils resist. This is clearly not likely to be a productive encounter. What is required is a way of breaking this logjam so that teacher and pupils can communicate across the apparently wide divide which separates them. Later on, we shall examine some strategies for bringing this about.

CHAPTER 2

Are children interested in death?

Many teachers think that children are not on the whole interested in the topic of death. Children are supposed to have their minds on more immediate and enjoyable events, and talking about death and dying with them would be far too gloomy to be acceptable. Why should we expect children who are beginning their lives to be particularly concerned about the nature of the end of those lives? One might expect people to think more about death the nearer they suppose themselves to be to it, and to talk to children about death while they are children seems rather peculiar. This is certainly how it appears to many teachers.

Yet when one talks to children about death one discovers a great deal of interest, and even fascination, with the topic. This is particularly the case with very young children, those in the pre-school, 3- to 5-year-old age range. It is surprising how readily such young children will talk about death. For them the phenomenon is often linked to particular animals or people with whom they have had close relationships, or in response to the sorts of stories they hear and read. The range of views they have is impressive. I was talking to a group of 4-year-olds in London about the death of animals, and they produced a variety of interpretations of the event:

> My dog died one day. He went to sleep, and we buried him. Got another dog now. He lives in the house, and the dead dog lives in the garden.

> My nan's dead. We don't see her any more. My mum cried. Where did nan go?

> When things die they go to sleep and they go away. Sometimes they come back. I don't know why.

> When it's dead you don't see it again. It has turned into something else.

The first child's statement was part of a much longer narration in which she said that the dog who now lived in the garden carried on doing the ordinary things which dogs do, but only at night when she could not see it. She was quite sure that even if she got up in the night to look for it she would not find it, and nor would anyone else, but she still insisted that it was dead. Her impression that it could get out of its grave and wander about had been strengthened for her by its having been buried in its favourite blanket, under the description of having gone to sleep. The difference between the dead dog and the new dog was that the former slept by day and the latter slept at night. Yet she also acknowledged that there was a distinction between falling asleep and dying, but could not say what it was. This is common among this age range.

The second child also did something which many others repeated. She started off by considering a dead animal, and immediately went on to talk about a dead person. Then she moved back to talking about animals. Children at this age will move freely from topic to topic, and there is evidence that they discuss these issues among themselves, although probably not for long periods. They were concerned about the where-abouts of the dead, and tend to regard as ridiculous the idea that a person could just go away forever. This then often gets linked with anxieties about what might happen to them should their parents go away or die, which is an anxiety which many children will explore, to a degree at least. Of course, some have had the experience of a parent leaving or dying, or have heard of it happening to others, and they tend to be very concerned at the impact which this will have on themselves. It would be interesting to be able to question young children about this at some length, but there are important ethical difficulties here. Many children exhibit signs of anxiety quite early on in such discussions, and it would be wrong to risk upsetting them by protracted questioning. One has to be very careful how one operates here. It may seem that children are talking quite freely and in a relaxed manner about death initially, and even by the end of the interview they may still appear to be happy and stimulated by the opportunity to present their views and explore their ideas. Yet afterwards they may become quite anxious, especially if they have been invited to think about the deaths of some of those close to them. While it is acceptable to listen to very young children and note down their conversations, they can in no real sense give their informed consent to being interviewed, and researchers have to bear this in mind when thinking about the boundaries of ethical investigation.

Children of this very young age have difficulty in understanding the physical processes related to death, and will often see death as being reversible. The processes of decomposition, or of transformation from one form into another after cremation, are difficult to grasp at this age, especially for urban children. It is worth distinguishing here between urban and rural children, because many of the latter will have been in a position to observe dead animals in various stages of decomposition and may have more awareness of what takes place in a body when it is dead. Rural children are less likely to think that death is reversible than urban children, but there is not otherwise much to distinguish them. One of the major sources of information for all children is the television, and on the television children see people and cartoon charac-ters being killed all the time, or totally mangled in some creative sort of way as with cartoon characters, and then if they ask what has happened to them, they are told that the character is not really dead. Parents will often explain to children that in a film with actors who have the role of being killed it is not really that they are going to be killed, but are only pretending. The actor will get up after the scene has been filmed, and go home. Now, one might wonder whether parents really discuss these sorts of topics with children, especially as they often put the children in front of the television to shut them up and occupy them while the adults get on with something else. But there is no doubt that even with this age group, watching television is often very much of a communal activity, and very young children may watch programmes which are designed for older people. These programmes may involve a good deal of death and dying presented in quite a graphic way, and it may even not be the work of actors, but it could be the news showing actual dead bodies, or people in hospital near death. Children will often ask parents to explain what is going on here, since if death is reversible, as they often think, they wonder why people make such a fuss about it. Will not the people who are lying in a heap on the ground with flies buzzing around eventually be able to get up and carry on with their normal activities? After all, this is what happens in the cartoons.

Since children are presented with so much contradictory information, it is hardly surprising that they become confused about how they are to think about death. Their confusion is only increased by the reluctance of their parents to discuss the issue. It is a common experience for parents to have children ask them questions about death, perhaps as a result of something they have seen on the television, and not know what to say in response. One of the interesting aspects of the sorts of questions which children of this age pose is that they are quite metaphysical. They are not just about the physical processes of death, but often touch on the nature of the relationship between life and death, and the way in which we should think about death. Parents will often brush off these questions and this is perhaps a shame, since their children are expressing an interest in some very basic issues concerning human beings and their role in the world. Parents feel, quite naturally, that they cannot enter into such issues with very young children, and perhaps this discourages children from exploring these ideas when they are older and better able to use the sorts of conceptual language which can deal with these topics. Another important motive for ignoring these questions, and changing the subject quickly, is that many adults see childhood as a time to avoid gloomy issues, a period in which children should be happy and amused. Talking about death seems to go against this. Parents might think that there will be plenty of time when the children are older to explore death, and so they avoid the topic in so far as they can.

Yet very young children are often interested in death, and as we have seen it is all around them as a result of the media. Conversations between such children will frequently touch on death, especially when one of the children has experienced the death of an animal or relative. The child will often want to talk about it, and if adults are unavailable or disinclined to discuss it with them, children will find an outlet somewhere else. When adults come across these conversations they often try to get the children to change the subject, claiming that they are talking about something which is 'morbid'. Modern parents are far more accepting of children talking about sex than they are about discussions of death – which indicates the replacement of an older taboo by a new one – although they are often not that keen on discussions about sex either. Perhaps one of the features about death which concerns parents and teachers of very young children is that the questions they are asked are so difficult to answer of their very nature. They raise interesting and perplexing issues which we find hard to understand ourselves as adults, let alone know how to discuss with children. Another feature which is certainly significant is the common attitude that the appropriate atmosphere in which very young children should develop is one of unceasing cheerfulness and optimism. There is a widespread feeling that these children should not be confronted with difficult and perplexing situations, and that everyone should be (or pretend to be) happy all the time. But children know that there are times when people are not happy, and that sometimes it is inappropriate to be cheerful. They themselves are frequently unhappy when things turn out awkwardly for them, and as they get towards the age of 5 they appreciate that their parents and teachers are not capable of sorting out all their problems.

This is why it is so important for them to receive an intelligent response when they ask questions about death, and the associated issues of loss and bereavement should not be ignored either. One of the reasons why very young children become interested in death is that they sense that this is an area beyond the control of adults. A lot of the questions they ask turn around this point, especially when it is an adult who dies. That apparently omnipotent adults can be obliged to die is a remarkable fact for children to confront. When these adults are close to the children a whole variety of emotions such as guilt, anxiety, fear and satisfaction may be involved, and it does not seem to be a good idea to try to ignore both the emotions and the facts of death just because the children involved are very young. It might be argued that they were at the age where it was most important to make sure that they have a vocabulary to discuss the issue, since they have such a relatively small background of experiences and knowledge upon which to draw. I would tentatively, suggest, then, that adults should be ready to discuss issues like death and loss with very young children. Those children should be encouraged to develop their ideas on the topic, and adults should not seek to disguise the painful and irreversible nature of death. That is not to say that adults should insist that children discuss such questions, but rather that when such questions arise they should not be ignored but should be taken up and form part of a discussion with the child in order to show him or her how death may be faced. It is no good adults pretending that everything is rosy all the time, not only because it is false but also because children know it is false. Since both adults and children know the same thing – that life sometimes is sad and there is nothing that can be done about it – one might think that this could serve as the basis of dialogue.

Older children in infant and primary schools often find death to be a less puzzling but possibly more worrying phenomenon. Some will have adopted a rather crude eschatology of heaven and hell, which helps at least to put death within some sort of context. Others will claim to be sceptical about such possibilities and are scathing about those who still believe them. These are some fairly typical responses:

Believing in heaven and hell is like believing in Father Christmas. When you die you die and never do anything else. (8-year-old boy)

When you die you go to heaven and you go to hell. It depends upon what you did when you were alive. My Dad says that Mrs Thatcher will go to hell, sure as anything. (9-year-old girl)

It's sad when someone dies. You don't see them any more. They get burnt up and turned into nothing. (10-year-old boy)

It is rather surprising that there is not much difference as children get older between denominational and non-denominational schools with respect to belief in heaven and hell. More children attending denominational schools believe in heaven and hell, but not so many more as one might expect, and as they near 11 and the end of primary schooling, the gap between the beliefs of children in the different schools narrows very rapidly. Children in non-denominational schools, however, do have a conception of an afterlife, sometimes religious and sometimes taking a different form, which they were often happy to discuss.

It might be expected that the reluctance of teachers to discuss death would not be present, or not to the same extent, among teachers in denominational schools. Of course, not all such teachers share the religious views of their schools, but there are plenty of Catholic and Anglican teachers who are firm believers and who are happy to attempt to pass on their beliefs to the children in their schools. These beliefs will include an attitude to the meaning of death, and teachers will explain what that meaning is and how it fits in with the rest of the religion. What beliefs will be discussed with pupils as the official doctrine of the Church? There still exists a stereotype of the religious school attempting to indoctrinate children in a very simple and clearcut notion of the afterlife, the character of which is strongly affected by the nature of our behaviour in this world. Believers are comforted with the thought that when they are dead they carry on in a more spiritual and perfect manner somewhere else, and they can help attain this new life through their activities while alive. This stereotype is not an accurate guide to much of the teaching which goes on within a religious context any more. Teachers within the Christian traditions of the Church of England and the Roman Catholic Church present a far more sophisticated model of the link between this life and the next. In particular, the character of the next life is described in far less vivid language than was the case in the past. One teacher spoke wistfully of the time when he was at a boys' Catholic secondary school and had to see the headmaster because of misbehaviour on his part. The head had a blazing fire in his study, and he placed the boy over it for a moment, informing him that this was merely a foretaste of the flames of hell which lay in wait for him unless he improved his behaviour! Such clear ideas about the afterlife are notably absent from contemporary schools, and a fairly apologetic doctrine about the nature of life after death is more often to be found.

No doubt this is an entirely praiseworthy reflection of the many theological and philosophical difficulties in the notion of a corporeal or spiritual afterlife, and it does have important implications for the teaching of death and dying as topics in the school. These are issues which even religious teachers and teachers of religion are often reluctant to explore, with the result that their pupils are not clearly prepared for this inevitable aspect of their lives. It is true, though, that teachers who claim adherence to a religion are able to produce more sophisticated and developed accounts of death and dying than their non-religious colleagues. These teachers are often in possession of quite firm beliefs not so much in the precise nature of the afterlife but in the purpose of death and dying, and their role in our lives. The main differences which comes out between the two groups of teachers (and it must be acknowledged that the religious/non-religious dichotomy is a very crude one and should really be represented as two ends of a continuum of views) is that the non-religious teacher is impressed by the apparent *absurdity* of the phenomenon of death. This feature makes it difficult for such teachers to discuss this phenomenon with their pupils, and indeed also with their colleagues and family. Most of the religious teachers I interviewed do not think that death is absurd, yet still find it difficult to discuss with their pupils. One reason is that they felt it important not to fall into trite platitudes. A rather typical response by a teacher in a Church of England primary school was:

We had this terrible case last year of two children in our school who were suddenly orphaned through a car accident. The pupils wanted to talk about why it had happened, and I did not know what to say. Obviously I would not want to say it was because God punished them. I suppose I would say that God wants us to be responsible for our own actions, and to have free will, and that these tragic events may play a part in his design which we cannot perceive ... But it sounds terribly platitudinous unless one shares my faith, and I wouldn't really know how to put it to the children.

The point he wished to make is that it would be wrong to produce a religious formula into which the event could neatly slot. It would not only be theologically wrong, but also it would not work with pupils.

This is more of a problem the older the pupils are. There is a role for quite simple stories in explanation of difficult religious points when one is working with very young children. They certainly would not understand more sophisticated language and when teaching one should use the form of explanation which is appropriate to the children's age. Accounts of an afterlife which involve heaven (given the common assumption that one should not upset or risk upsetting children, the notion of hell is usually omitted) are popular with young children, as is the notion of God living in the sky and the dead going to live with him up there. The time comes, though, when these stories no longer convince, and it is necessary to switch to a more appropriate description of an afterlife. For many children this stage occurs at about the same time as the loss of faith in the existence of Father Christmas. But we should beware of assuming that children's development of the notions of death and the afterlife progresses smoothly. Some children find it impossible at any stage of their lives to accept the traditional view of an afterlife, with dead people going on somewhere else to 'live with Jesus', while others find this perfectly easy to accept and will carry it with them forever. Yet it is also a mistake to think of very young children, even pre-school infants, as incapable of quite sophisticated discussion of the topics of death and the afterlife. Many teachers and parents have been driven almost round the bend by the acute interrogation of a very young child when the latter is expected to accept a religious platitude. Some children are very reluctant to do so, and they will persistently demand of the adult, and of their peers, an explanation which they can find intellectually satisfactory. We shall give some examples of such conversations later, but it is worth saying here that it is dangerous to relate age to the sort of questions and answers which will stimulate and satisfy children *simpliciter*. There is a diversity in the response of the child which teachers and parents would do well to respect.

Teachers in secondary schools are also worried about how to talk with children about death from a religious perspective. There is a widespread belief among teachers that many of the children in such schools, however religious they are formally, do not believe in the main principles of the school's religion, and so would find it difficult to accept the sort of account of death which requires faith in order to be persuasive. Some parents send their children to denominational schools because they think they are good schools, and not to further their religious adherence to a particular faith. The parents may themselves be quite sceptical, and may take steps to ensure that the child does not accept everything which the school propounds concerning religion. Besides, there is an ethic in many such schools of presenting religion in as positive and cheerful a light as possible. Religion has to be shown to be fun, and religious people do not have to be presented as solemn and serious people all the time. As a result, the topics of death and dying are often rejected as too gloomy for young people. Religious teachers are often persuaded that discussing death with their pupils would put them off religion, and that children are not on the whole interested in this topic. Children are perceived as young (which they certainly are) and carefree (which they might be), and so religion has to partake of these characteristics if it is to be attractive. There is no doubt that talking to children about death and dying goes rather against this emphasis, and is therefore avoided if at all possible.

It is perhaps surprising that this attitude should persist so long into secondary schooling. Children of secondary school age may entertain complex views on death, buttressed by a degree of experience which has often been thoroughly assimilated by the young person. Most of the children in this age range will have personal experience of someone close to them who has died. They will have considered issues of death in school through their reading matter and work with teachers. They should have acquired a more sophisticated view of themselves and of the nature of the experiences of others. One is often impressed by the sensitivity of expression and the intelligence of their approach to the topic of death. Even children at the early stages of secondary school are capable of producing interesting material on this issue. They will themselves say that as they get older they see death as more of a personal issue, rather than as just something which affects someone else. Expressions of personal anxiety only became marked on a relatively large scale when young people start to identify more with adults than with children. As one might expect, there is a huge variety of points of view about death, and there is little point in trying to push them into neat categories. Certain common themes are worth exploring, though, since they have something to tell us about how ideas about death develop at this stage.

Some adolescents are very unreflective about death, even though they are curious about other important aspects of humanity, while others produce sophisticated descriptions of what is involved in dying and yet display little understanding of broader issues. The important variable here is experience. There are adolescents who have come into frequent contact with death, and sometimes this contact has been traumatic and of major significance in their lives. As we have seen, class enters the picture here, since more working-class children are likely to come into contact with death than are their middle-class peers. When the nature of death is violent, more boys are likely to be involved than girls. At the moment Britain is a relatively non-violent society, and many adolescents will never have witnessed a violent incident. There are some, though, who inhabit a persistently dangerous and violent sub-culture where death and injury are common events. There is a tendency to think of such children as hardened and coarse criminals, who have lost the capacity to think about the interests of others and who behave callously in what they regard as the furtherance of their ends. Yet this is often far from the case. Young people who are involved in violent activities are frequently able to express complex and sensitive views about what they do, and it is important for them to take the prospect of death seriously, since it is always at the rim of their lives in a more direct sense than in the case of more peaceful life-styles. They have collected the sorts of experiences during their lives upon which they can reflect, and they do reflect on them in many instances.

Take as an example a young man of 17 in London who had recently left school and whose career at school had been frequently interrupted by expulsions and truancy. Since his time in primary school he had been involved in violent crime of one kind or another, graduating from bullying to mugging and extortion. When I met him he was no longer a petty criminal but had been 'reformed' as a result of finding a cause – right-wing politics – and was widely suspected of being part of a gang which carried out assaults on Asians in the East End. Although the police had questioned him many times, he had managed to avoid being charged. He had no compunction about referring to violent incidents in which he had been involved, since this gave him status within his peer group, but he presumably was not so frank with the police! When asked about the feelings of those whom he attacked he replied:

Of course they have feelings, just like we do. But what you have to realize is that a war is going on here, and in war people get hurt. Life is a matter of conflict, you've got to get on top, since if you don't someone will get on top of you, and if you are too slow, they will knife you or worse. We've got to show them who is boss. When you get into a fight you have to forget about the feelings of the other person, since if you get weak, they will win. When I run away after hurting someone I just feel excited, because I know that they would have hurt me if they could. Later on, though, I sometimes wonder about it all. But they started it by coming over here and taking over our area, and they deserve everything they get . . . I could easily get killed or arrested for what I do, but I think it's worth it.

We can link this with the apparently reckless behaviour of teenagers who get involved in sexual intercourse without taking precautions against HIV infection. A 14-year-old girl in Manchester explained:

I just cannot be bothered with all that AIDS stuff. If you catch it you catch it and there is nothing you can do about it. You can get killed crossing the road, or something can drop on your head. It's all down to chance. How things end up is not down to you, so you might as well enjoy yourself while you can and not worry about it.

This sort of fatalism is quite common among adolescents who admit to being involved in what might be thought of as risky behaviour. This form of explanation for behaviour is extremely common when teenagers are asked about smoking.

How should we regard such responses? A tempting suggestion is that we should condemn them, or at the very least criticize them, and point out to the young people involved that what they are doing is, at the very least, harmful to their own interests. We might also want to say that they are morally wrong, but teachers quite rightly worry about how effective such an approach might be. What teachers are on the whole very ready to attack are ways of living which they perceive as harmful, and they will often seek to convince the pupils involved in such activities of the error of their ways. Yet it is worth noting something very important about the attitudes of these young people, and that is that they have thought seriously about their own death and are well aware that they are acting in ways which may hasten it. We may not approve of the attitudes which they have to their lives and to their deaths, but we do have to accept that they have thought about things which many of their teachers and other adults do not think about. These young people have had experiences which involve death and injury, and they know that the courses of action which they are undertaking are likely to lead to an end the nature of which they are prepared to consider.

This might seem to be a crude misinterpretation of the facts. Surely, it will be said, what many young people are doing in expressing fatalistic views is denying death. They are saying that they are going to behave in rather dangerous ways despite the consequences, which involves defending themselves from the personal implications of their actions. It certainly is remarkable how many grandparents one hears referred to as hale and hearty in old age despite a lifetime's proclivity for untipped cigarettes! In some ways it is comforting to reflect that whatever steps one might take to preserve one's life, one's fate is really out of one's own hands. After all, one can drop dead at any time, and people do. This is an especially comforting thought if one is contemplating rather reckless behaviour. What should be noted here, though, is that this sort of fatalism is not necessarily an attempt at avoiding the likely consequences of one's actions. It can also be an acknowledgement that those actions are likely to end in death, in a death which has been evaluated and put within a wider context. The young people concerned understand that the death which lies at the end of life is going to happen to them, and so they do not fall foul of Ivan Ilych's fallacy. This, it will be recalled, is his realization that he will die because he is mortal, but it does not provide a conclusion which he applies to himself. As Tolstoy puts it, 'The syllogism he had learnt... "Caius is a man, men are mortal, therefore Caius is mortal" had always seemed to him correct as applied to Caius, but certainly not as applied to himself' (Tolstoy, 1960, p. 131). Ivan Illych was not a fatalist. He had just not connected the omnipresence and inevitability of mortality with himself. He was wrong not to do so, since, as he knew from his early work in logic, his death inevitably and necessarily followed from his having lived. This mistake is not made by those who make the choice to live dangerously. They understand what could well be in store for them as a result of their activities.

How far is this an accurate picture of the thinking of the majority of these young people? When one looks at a young man with a skinhead haircut, with fascist tattoos on his arms and an arrogant expression on his face it is difficult to conceive of his having thought at some length about his own death. When one sees a young woman smoking a lot of cigarettes and not apparently taking any serious steps to preserve her physical well-being, one might say that she has ignored the consequences of her actions. This is particularly the case if she gets involved in a lot of activities which are potentially harmful and which will in all likelihood shorten her life. It is difficult to think of these people as having deliberately worked out the course of action which they are following and which they fully understand. One is tempted to think that they have been drawn into their behaviour by powerful social forces, perhaps by the power of advertising or through the influence of important individuals. Their behaviour seems to be the very opposite of autonomous. Nonetheless, it is undoubtedly true that many such young people have seriously thought through their actions, and they have a firm view of the nature of the death which they might hasten through those actions. Teachers may well think that it is their responsibility to warn their pupils of the likely consequences of their actions, and they will belabour young people with the risks they are taking. Ironically, it is the young people who have a clearer idea of their actions than their teachers, for adolescents and teenagers will probably come across youngsters like themselves who have suffered as a result of their behaviour, or they will have heard about such cases.

But is it not the case that the risks are not properly understood by the young people involved, or that they deny the consequences of their actions? Of course, it is possible that both these factors come into the picture, and yet it is also true that young people themselves are in a position to know a lot more about their activities than their teachers. For one thing, it is the young people themselves who are carrying out those activities, and they know about them from the point of view of direct acquaintance. They are practitioners and not observers, and there is a knowledge of practice which is only really available to the former. This is not to say that they understand all aspects of what they are doing, since there is clearly a level of knowledge which belongs to the outsider who perhaps knows more about the context within which the agents' activities take place than the agents themselves. Teachers may understand better the sorts of pressure under which young people are labouring, since adults may be able to remove themselves to a certain extent from those pressures once they have passed the age when they are most acute. They are able to stand back from those pressures and observe them with a certain detachment, while young people are in the thick of them. So the expertise which teachers have to bring to the situation is an expertise due to greater experience and a more objective view of the situation, which leads to a greater awareness of the risks involved.

We should be very careful about accepting this analysis of the situation, though. Risk is in many ways a social concept, and assessments will vary in accordance with a whole range of personal and cultural factors. If an individual decides that he or she will take a course of action despite the fact that it may shorten life expectancy, there is no objective assessment of risk which applies to everyone. We may misunderstand the degree of risk involved, but there is no degree of risk which means that the action should not be undertaken. It is up to the agent to decide, and if the agent is prepared to acknowledge and take the risk, then this is an example of free decision-making. It is certainly not true that as a society we disapprove of risky activities, since there are many dangerous activities which receive high public praise and reward. One only has to think here of some sports and of the behaviour of the armed services, police and fire brigade. Through their actions they run quite a high risk of death or injury, yet we applaud what they do, even when, as in the case of mountaineers, what they do has no public benefit as a justification. Who is to say that when young people decide to smoke they are accepting a risk which is greater than they should accept? If they understand the consequences, then they are accepting a degree of risk which is acceptable *for them*. The implication often seems to be that if young people really knew what the risks are, they would never get involved in the dangerous activities which do sometimes attract them, and it is appropriate for teachers to inform them of those risks. But in many cases young people already understand the nature of the risks. It is their teachers who are terrified of the risks, and we should turn our attention to the attitudes of teachers if we are to understand more precisely the nature of confrontation between them and their pupils on the nature of risk.

CHAPTER 3

Teachers and attitudes to death

Teachers are very risk-averse people on the whole. This is a point which must be grasped before we can make sense of the ways in which teachers discuss risk, and the forms of death which are associated with it. There is evidence that teachers find the notion of death a particularly hard one to accept. Teachers are themselves part of a system which is characterized by a progression of the child towards greater knowledge and skill, and the idea that this suddenly comes to an end is difficult to accept. Teachers managed to get through the various educational hoops when they were at school, and they later leap or crawl through similar hoops at college and during their training. Then they spend much of the rest of their professional lives trying to help their pupils succeed in the educational system. The structure of teaching and learning itself, the notion of a curriculum with its grades and of a hierarchy with its ranks and promotions, encourages the idea that life consists of a series of stages and obstacles which must be surmounted if one is to be successful. Of course, not everyone can enjoy the same level of success, but it is felt to be important that everyone try to succeed and reach the level of attainment they are capable of. The Puritan ethic is certainly alive and well in the staffrooms of Britain, and teachers will constantly exhort their pupils to work hard if they wish to succeed in life, as they themselves have worked hard to reach a certain position in society.

It would be wrong to think that this view of life as a series of hoops and obstacles to overcome if one is to play one's full part is restricted to teachers, nor is it necessarily part of the psychological background of all teachers. It became clear in the course of my research on attitudes to death that teachers do in many cases possess a strong belief in life as a process replete with difficulties to be overcome. A fairly representative view is that of Joyce, a 35-year-old teacher in London, who described to me her view of life:

> Well, I had to work hard to get where I am today, which is not to say that I am anywhere very important. I had to do well at school and then get adequate grades at 'A' Level to go to college. While

there I had to complete an enormous number of assignments as well as survive teaching practice in a series of really grotty schools. In my first job I found it very difficult to get the children to do anything at all, and had to think hard about how I was going to approach them every day. Now that I have more experience and am a year head I am much more relaxed, yet I expect that with the recent changes in the education system I shall have to put more work into the new things I shall have to do . . . I think it is important for children and teachers to work hard in school. I often say to the children that all they have to do if they wish to get on is work hard and not let the opportunities go past them, but many of them don't . . . I think teachers have to put a lot of effort into their work in school. The days when one could just relax and teach your subject are dead and gone. Teachers will have to be a lot clearer about what they are doing and why, and will have to restrict themselves to relatively narrow activities . . . My view of death? Well, I don't really have a view. I don't believe in an afterlife or anything like that. I think that this is all we have, and then we die and everything stops for us. I suppose that is all that one can say . . . I suppose, when you think about it, the fact that everything comes to an end in death makes everything a bit futile.

It may seem remarkably crude to summarize the views of a whole group of teachers with a report of a conversation with just one, but it is interesting that Joyce's comments are so representative of secular teachers. Very few teachers interviewed were prepared to say anything much more detailed about death. Even teachers with religious beliefs were often unable to say much more, with the exception of a small but significant group of teachers whom we shall consider in due course.

Teachers often see themselves as reflective people, and it is surprising that they seem to reflect so little about death. In fact, this seems to be quite characteristic of those in more middle-class occupations. When one discusses death with those in working-class occupations one comes across far more complex views, which are also much closer to the nature of their occupations and to their experiences. It is worth recalling here how the statistics of death and injury replicate the class system, in that the lower down the social scale one goes, the higher the level of early death and disability, due both to the nature of the work and to life-style. When those in working-class occupations were asked to list close friends and relatives who had died it was clear that they could compile a longer list than their more middle-class contemporaries. Those in working-class occupations could name more colleagues who had died at work, and also those who had been disabled through industrial accidents, than middle-class people. In conversation, perhaps as a result, working-class respondents had a much better defined notion of death. It was clearly something they had thought about, and many of them had relatively sophisticated views on the nature of death and its role in our lives.

In some ways this seems rather surprising. We tend to think of working-class people as being less sophisticated in their use of language and therefore less conceptual in their thinking than middle-class people. Indeed, at one time it was quite common to attribute differences in the performance of working- and middle-class pupils to the different sorts of language which they heard at home. Middle-class occupations put a premium on language skills and on conceptual sophistication, by contrast with many working-class occupations, and it is not unnatural to expect the latter to be less competent in their use of the language than the former. This is not to suggest that working-class people are unable to speak decent English, but only that they spend less time developing a complex linguistic facility, tending to use simpler and more direct expressions, and that their reading matter is thinner conceptually than is the case with the middle class. Yet the suggestion here seems to be that what in fact happens with respect to language about death is that the normal relationship between the classes is reversed. The working-class respondents are much more likely to engage in detailed discussions of the role of death in their lives, and will report on deaths with which they are acquainted. A 41-year-old building worker in Liverpool commented:

> For the first few years I went onto sites I never got a scratch. I saw people have accidents, mind, and one of my best friends broke his back falling off scaffolding. But you know what it's like when you are a youngster, you don't think anything is going to happen to you. But over the years so many of my mates have had accidents, it makes you think. One minute there you are, happy as a lark on top of the world, and the next you are dead or worse. And believe me, it's worse to be seriously injured, to be crippled or have your insides mangled by a digger. I'm dead careful now, and I've turned down work which I thought was dangerous, even though I really needed it. You know, when you work on building sites you realize that you are lucky just to be alive, to be able to get up in the morning.

A factory worker in Yorkshire said:

> I wouldn't say it was dangerous here, not like in the past. But I'm 56 now and I've seen some things in my time. Two good friends were killed in one year. I still dream about them and wonder what they would be doing now if they were still alive. One of them spent all his time going out with lasses, and I suppose he had the right idea. At least he enjoyed himself while he could, he pushed as much as he could into his life. That's what we should all do.

These short extracts from long discussions about the deaths of friends and colleagues exhibited a high level of thought about what death meant and what implications that meaning has for the way we live.

Now, when one examines these and other comments, one is not impressed by the depth of the insights which the interviewees produced. Often they produced familiar platitudes and truisms about death. What is interesting about these discussions is that individuals were prepared to speak at length about death, and about the effects of the deaths with which they have come into contact, on their lives. They had clearly connected the phenomenon of death with their own lives, and they had developed an attitude to it. Although these individuals are on the whole less confident users of sophisticated English than their middle-class contempories, within the confines of their linguistic abilities they did express clearly defined views on death. This was obviously something that they had thought about for some time. Now, it has to be admitted that it is difficult to assess how far people think about a topic just from listening to what they have to say about it. Some people can no doubt think long and hard about something without expressing themselves in such a way as to give that impression. It is commonplace for teachers to notice that some pupils are quick to answer questions and comment on topics without having really thought clearly about what they are saying, while others will be reluctant to speak but may have a lot of interesting things to contribute. On the other hand, if a group of professionals, in this case teachers, exhibit reluctance to talk about an issue, while another group, here manual workers, is ready and eager to talk about it, one is not making a wild assumption about differences in their attention to the topic if one suggests that the former group is in possession of less developed ideas about the topic, and that they have not thought how to relate that topic to their own existences.

We need to remind ourselves here of the differences between attitudes to the future held by different social classes. It was argued that middle-class perceptions of work tend to see it as highly structured and logical in form, which contrast with working-class perceptions. It is not improbable that this difference in perception leads also to a distinction in conceptions of the nature of life itself, since our notion of our work is often an important aspect of our idea of life. As we have seen, working-class reactions to risk are often quite different from middle-class reactions, in that working-class people may emphasize the random nature of fate and so not find it surprising that lives are sometimes cut off before old age. We have also argued that in contemporary society there is a good deal of evidence of the denial of death, which has lead to a decline in the paraphernalia surrounding death and dying, and in turn has helped create a taboo out of death. We need to be aware of class differences here too. It may be that there are significant differences between attitudes to death along class lines. This comes out in a number of ways. In the interviews which were conducted as part of the research for this book, far more working-class respondents had thought about what they wanted for their funerals, and had made specific financial provision for it. They had often thought about what they wanted to have inscribed on the tombstone, and they had thought about whether they wanted to be buried or cremated. There is evidence of quite extended discussion on this topic, and many respondents had definite views. By contrast, few middle-class respondents had considered it at all, and were happy to leave it to their relatives to decide. Nor did they approve of elaborate and extended rituals connected with funerals or cremation, while the working-class replies often touched on the importance of a 'good send off', and many comparisons were made between different funerals and the subsequent wake or meeting in a house or public place to commemorate the deceased. This was often seen as very important, and many working-class respondents were able to go into detail about what they hoped would be done for them.

It is quite common for people to leave flowers and other tributes at the spot where a tragedy took place, or at a place where that tragedy is commemorated. This is often ritualized, as during Armistice Day and its celebration with poppies and wreaths of flowers. More informally, though, when children in particular have been run over, or a popular adult figure has been killed, people who may not have known the individuals concerned will come and leave flowers with an inscription. It would be interesting to know what the occupational background of these mourners is, and although it would be far too insensitive to ask, some information can be picked up by examining the writing on the tributes and noting the clothing and transport of the visitors to the spot. They appear to be predominantly working-class, and the need to mark a tragedy in this way is a reflection of working-class culture. The idea that death should be marked by tributes, and that a public demonstration should be made of grief even for people unknown to oneself, is much more commonly held by working-class than by middle-class respondents. I remember how reactions differed to the public outpouring of grief in Liverpool after the events at Hillsborough in 1989. Many supporters of Liverpool Football Club had been killed during the collapse of part of the stand in Sheffield, and these were predominantly young men, many of whom were still at school. The enormous number of wreaths which were left at Anfield, carpeting a large area of ground, were added to day after day. A memorial has now been erected there, but before this happened it became something of a place of pilgrimage. The public reacted to this display of grief in different ways. Working-class respondents were entirely in favour of the display, seeing it as moving and appropriate, a genuine mark of respect for the dead.

There is a tendency in Britain for rituals surrounding death to be influenced by class. When one walks around a modern cemetery it is not difficult to guess the social position of those buried there by looking at the tombstones. It is too simple to say that the most elaborate are necessarily working-class, but on the whole one can fairly successfully predict the sort of families they came from. Cultural factors are important here too, in that British families of Irish origin may still maintain the more exuberant and ceremonial rituals surrounding death that one finds in Ireland. Irish families often like to have a photograph of the deceased on the stone itself, and the rituals accompanying a funeral are quite protracted and elaborate. A lot of discussion will go into the events of the funeral and its associated activities, and there is a clearly defined notion of what constitutes a 'good sending off'. Relatives would be criticized if they did not arrange an appropriate ritual to commemorate the burial (or very occasionally cremation), and there are high expectations among members of the community regarding what a funeral should be and how it should be conducted. Middle-class attitudes to funerals, by contrast, are more restrained. They include a brief service, with little fuss made to commemorate the occasion. Explicit grief behaviour is frowned upon, and an attempt is made to get the business over with as quickly as possible. Again, it is difficult to generalize, but from personal observation it often seems that middle-class participants at a funeral are less sure of their roles than are working-class mourners.

When individuals from different social groups were asked about the rituals surrounding funerals they gave very different answers. Working-class respondents were often happy to describe in detail what they would like to happen at their own funerals, who they would want to come, even down to the kind of food and drink which they wanted served afterwards. They had definite views on the desirability of either burial or cremation, and they wanted a certain number of visits to be made to their grave or, where relevant, commemorative stone. Middle-class respondents had on the whole little to contribute on any of these topics. One comment which was often made was that they disapproved of elaborate displays of either emotion or expense. This was clearly shown by middle-class respondents' shock, during the Hillsborough commemoration at Anfield, at the enormous number of wreaths and bouquets of flowers. Their reaction at the time was often to criticize such a display as 'mawkish', 'bad taste' and 'over the top'. There is no reason to think that this response was linked to the fact that football is predominantly a working-class game, or that most of the dead and injured were working-class themselves. It is probably true that middle-class people were just as upset by the events as working-class people, and that the emotional atmosphere was felt equally strongly by both social groups. Where they differed was in what they considered to be an appropriate response. A restrained response was felt by the middle class to be in good taste, whereas the exuberant and extravagant marking of the tragedy at Anfield was felt to be in the very worst of taste. Even at times when a whole community shares a great sense of grief, the different social groups of that community do not share the same idea of how that grief should be expressed. It would be strange if it were otherwise, since social divisions affect a whole range of cultural events and how they are marked.

It might be thought that matters of taste were really too trivial to play much part in our understanding of how different sections of society regard death and bereavement, but this would be a mistake. Taste as it relates to conduct is an extremely important indicator of deeper social divisions, for while the areas of behaviour which are governed by taste might well be seen as trivial, what they reveal is very far from being trivial. A good example of this can be seen by contrasting the approaches which different newspapers take in dealing with disasters and tragedies. What tends to happen is that agencies and individual photographers send in a series of interesting photographs relating to the event, and the decision has to be taken whether to use them, and where to place them in the paper. These photographs may show grieving parents and children, dead or dying people and scenes of a gruesome nature. A number of points arise here, such as whether the people in the photograph have given their permission to be photographed and whether they have a moral right to privacy. Putting these questions to one side for the moment, since they do not concern us here, one question remains for the editor – whether or not he should use such representations of death and grief. Even if the subjects have given permission, do the paper's readers want to see such pictures? This is an important consideration for the editor, since the readers pay for the newspaper and may go elsewhere if they become dissatisfied with their product.

In the more popular newspapers there are often many graphic representations of death and grief, and there will be frequent reference to funerals, to sobbing relatives and distraught friends. Blood-curdling scenes will be presented in graphic detail, often now in colour. The text will follow the pictures. Reporters will be interested in interviews which probe the feelings of the bereaved, and there will be extensive descriptions of the emotions of all concerned. All in all, a highly dramatic picture will be provided of the incident and its aftermath, and the feelings of participants and survivors will be explored in some detail. The broadsheet press tends to behave rather differently. Although these sorts of incidents are indeed reported, and often accompanied by pictures, they will be given less emphasis than in the more popular press. Editors will decide what sorts of pictures are suitable for their readership, and often the most graphic representations of grief and death are deemed unsuitable for publication. Of course, such editorial discretion may apply not only to major tragedies, but also to a whole range of events, including sexual misdemeanours and public scandals. Different kinds of newspaper will opt for different sorts of coverage. What I wish to focus on here are particular kinds of events, those which directly involve loss of life and the feelings of survivors and relatives. When the broadsheets do print pictures of grieving relatives and friends, or graphic representations of the incident itself, they often receive letters from readers complaining about the insensitivity and bad taste of publishing such photographs. Readers will also complain about any articles which appear in the paper about such events. Since the readership of these papers is predominantly middle-class, we are justified in thinking that this is a middle-class reaction to representations of death and grief. They see as inappropriate a style of coverage which is, in fact, commonplace in the popular press.

Why? When the broadsheets overstep the mark, in the view of some of their readers, this results in bad taste (let us assume for now that issues of invasion of privacy do not also arise). It is important that readers be made aware of the terrible things which happen as they happen, and such events should be reported, but it is often felt by many regular readers that there are limits to how they are to be reported and what sort of details are made available to the public. This applies not just to tragic events, but to a whole range of what might be regarded as dramatic incidents, and yet this disinclination to peer closely at a wide range of such events is highly revealing of the middle-class psyche. The reporting of these incidents will concentrate on the bare details and then go into some depth on how they came about and how they might be prevented in the future. The events will be analysed in rather instrumental terms, and an attempt will be made to avoid playing on the emotions of the public in connection with them. In fact, the buyer of

The Times, Independent and *Guardian* will smile contemptuously at the lurid headlines and pictures which are glimpsed on the front pages of the tabloid press.

How do the readers of the tabloid press justify their interest in the detailed description of tragedies, down to the physical events themselves and to the reactions of the main survivors or relatives? This reply by a refuse collector in Birmingham is typical:

> It is interesting to find out what went on, I mean, everything that happened, since you often think it could happen to you. Take a big smash-up on the motorway. Well, that could happen to anyone. Or when a dog savages a child, that could happen anytime to my kids. I suppose I think when I read about it, I wonder what it would be like if it happened to me . . . And when there is stuff about the relatives and that, I wonder what I'd do in that situation, how I'd cope. It makes you realise how lucky you are not to have these things happen to you, but they could, and you have to think about that too. I don't just want the facts – they're boring – but I want to know what people did about it afterwards, how they felt.

This respondent was a male of 29, and many tabloid readers of both sexes said much the same. There was a difference between male and female readers, in that men tended to look for more of what might be called the 'gory details', while women were more interested in the 'personal interest' angle. What is of interest in the reaction of both men and women is that they often stressed the importance of relating the event and its aftermath to themselves, either as a warning of what might easily happen to them or as an indication of how they themselves might respond to it as a survivor or relative. The 'personal interest' story was taken to be interesting precisely because it was personal, and many readers were able to empathize with the feelings and reactions of both the victims and their friends and relatives.

This was emphasized when the suggestion was made that representations of the deaths and subsequent grief constituted 'prying', a frequent response by readers of the broadsheet press. Some respondents did accept that journalists could be insensitive, and that people did have a right to privacy, but on the whole most people thought that this right was outweighed by the importance of the public at large knowing about what went on and how the survivors had reacted to the disaster. The point was made many times that what had happened to the people in the event might have happened to the readers, and was therefore personally relevant. Not only did it help the readers to put themselves in the place of both the dead and the bereaved, it also enabled them to discuss the event in some detail, since that detail had been provided by the press. This supports the idea that working-class readers use their newspapers and magazines to support and construct a complicated vocabulary which is appropriate to discuss death, dying and bereavement. Hence they are able to carry out such discussions in some detail and in a way which relates those discussions to the lives and experiences of the readers themselves. This linking of the reality of death as represented through the media with the lives of the readers comes up often when they talk about death and bereavement, since they bring up examples from the newspapers or the other media to help illustrate their points, and to indicate the practical ways in which they have been affected by the news.

Middle-class readers, by contrast, tend to ignore these topics of discussion, and where they do arise they fail to relate them to themselves. As we have seen, the nature of the news coverage they are exposed to supports their disinclination to relate it to themselves in a personal manner. They seek to adopt an objective view of the event, as opposed to the more subjective attitude of the popular press and its readers. When one asks individuals about their attitude to such events one has to try to interpret what might be fairly guarded and ambiguous replies in order to work out what sort of attitude is held by them. This is an inevitable aspect of research in social science, but it is worth also looking at the sorts of attitudes which are implicit in the media, directed as these are at specific groups in our society. The success or failure of vast commercial enterprises depends upon the editors of the media getting it right. Presenting a more objective or subjective view to the wrong audience constitutes a commercial risk, and one assumes that media proprietors take extensive steps to avoid damage to their circulation. This is not to suggest that readers follow their newspapers' approach sheepishly. Obviously they do not, and are often critical of what they read and see in their papers. The public is often aware of the ways in which the media try to manipulate them, and they are capable of ignoring large chunks of what they are reading and seeing as well. The suggestion here is not that different groups in society are led to adopt certain attitudes to death and bereavement by their adherence to particular publications. The relationship between attitudes and the media is far more subtle. The media support and often extend the attitudes which their readers already possess. Readers find within the press ideas and approaches with which they already concur, and they use these to elaborate the attitudes which they find acceptable.

How does this affect the attitudes of teachers to death? As we have seen, there is good reason to think that teachers are especially anxious about death themselves. If it is true that middle-class people tend to avoid the topic and are reluctant to deal with it, then this supports the notion that teachers, as members of the middle class, are likely to adopt this attitude. It would be interesting to know how occupational activities related to attitudes to death, and it might well be seen that there was a close correlation. It is not unlikely to be the case, since it might be thought that a particular attitude to death formed part of the personality of the individual choosing certain kinds of work, and that that work then went on to deepen the attitude. It would appear, then, that teachers are in a particularly difficult position when it comes to discussing death and associated topics, and that they should examine this position and seek to change it.

It might seem that I am blithely lumping the great variety of teachers together and making wild and unsubstantiated claims about a huge workforce based upon interviews and observations of just a few of them. Whether the respondents in the survey are truly representative of the profession as a whole is difficult to establish, but it will have to be left to others to decide whether the picture of the personality of the teacher which has been constructed on the basis of these interviews and the social context in which teachers live and work are persuasive. Clearly there are some teachers who are very interested in issues relating to death, and they may participate in Cruse and other organizations devoted to the counselling of bereaved individuals. These may be the teachers who are called upon by their schools when pupils are having problems coping with a bereavement, or when a disaster strikes. The argument here is that most teachers are even more reluctant to get involved in this area of discussion than other members of the public, and that they share the disinclination of the middle class to explore their own feelings about death in any detail or to any depth.

I argued earlier that it is an error to think that children in denominational schools are likely to have very different attitudes to death compared with children in secular schools. We need to distinguish between three kinds of teacher. Secular teachers often regard death as absurd, as cutting off people from life for no particular reason, and they find it a difficult topic to investigate. Death, especially the death of a child, reveals the educational process to be just that, a process, and any process can be disrupted through the intervention of arbitrary forces. It indicates the problematic nature of seeking to help children to get to a further stage which may suddenly be made unavailable to them through death. Teachers without religious beliefs may find this difficult to reconcile with their own professional motivation, and may exhibit considerable anxiety when contemplating death. Teachers with religious convictions do at least have both a ritual and a set of beliefs which give death a place in the scheme of things. A particular death may be difficult to accept, but there will be a full-blooded theological system which provides a context within which that death can be comprehended. As we have seen, this is a difficult matter to put across to pupils, who are only willing to accept simplistic accounts of an afterlife while quite young. Yet there will be some system in place which is designed to mark death, and it is often comforting in situations of emotional tension to be able to lean on such institutional supports, whether in the form of physical structures such as buildings and vestments, or through prayer and a particular ritual which needs to be employed. Teachers who adhere to religious principles often say how comforting they are when they need to cope with problems arising from bereavement, and religious schools can at the very least try to go through a religious form of ceremony which places the death within a broader context.

One of the points worth making about such teachers in denominational schools is that even when they are formal members of a particular church, this does not imply that they necessarily share a total faith in the teachings of that church or in the church's teaching on death and the afterlife. They may have a deep faith in the church and its teachings, and they may not. They may feel that they have to work out for themselves what their attitude to death ought to be. But there *is* a group of teachers who have no problem in putting death within a religious perspective, and this consists of those teachers who are part of the evangelical movement. They have very firm beliefs about the nature of death and the afterlife, and they have no difficulties whatsoever in accepting a fairly simple view of these matters. This is in no way to disparage their beliefs, but they do see the connection between the character of this life and the afterlife as being quite easy to understand, and they are often happy to accept a model of the afterlife which is quite graphic in detail and closely related in some important aspects to what goes on in this life. Ironically, many of these teachers do not work within denominational schools, since they would often not feel comfortable within their ambit. Their teaching of religious subjects would be restrained in church schools since they would be expected to follow the main principles of whichever church was maintaining it. While some Church of England schools might embrace evangelical ideas, the evangelical teachers themselves would probably feel that they could not really express themselves properly within such an environment. After all, denominational schools have advisors who monitor the nature of the curriculum and there are texts which teachers are supposed to use. Many evangelical Christians would find those advisors and texts far too watered-down in their approach to religion, and would seek to replace them with other texts and attempt to establish a more direct link to the deity.

Most of these evangelical teachers work, then, in the non-denominational sector, and they give the children in their classes a very strict religious education, including very firm views on the nature of life and death. Their influence is strongest at the junior level, of course, and they may infuse their form of Christianity into the curriculum by using a lot of religious examples and telling a good many religious stories. This leads to the rather paradoxical situation that there are cities in Britain with denominational schools which are turning out children with far less firm religious beliefs than the non-denominational schools in the same area. The number and influence of such teachers is not significant. There are probably not a lot of them, and they would only have a child in their class for a year or so, so their impact upon the child is probably not very great either. What is interesting about them is what they demonstrate by contrasting with the teachers in the denominational schools. The latter are guarded and cautious in their presentation of religion. The evangelicals are neither of these things, they are supremely confident and able to communicate a simple message. Death plays an important part in that message, and they would encourage pupils to think about the nature of the end of life and how they are going to prepare for it.

A picture is building up of the teacher as perhaps the very worst person to deal with issues connected with death. Teachers as a group exhibit anxiety when talking about death, and as members of the middle class are disinclined to talk about death anyway. Since teaching is very much a future-orientated activity, it leads to placing a lot of emphasis on the future, and when that future includes something which destroys it, death, we seem to be faced with a phenomenon which sucks all the meaning out of the activity. Now, as things stand at the moment teachers will not usually have to confront the topic of death directly in school, but it will come in indirectly when teachers discuss those activities with their pupils which they regard as far too risky to be acceptable. This is just one aspect of what may be wrong with these activities, of course, since it is also important to stress (if such is the case) that they are often against the law. There are many things which young people wish to do and which teachers wish them not to do, and to avoid being morally prescriptive teachers will often stress the danger inherent in those activities, and will try to dissuade youngsters from pursuing them. Yet the pupils themselves will often have a different concept of what constitutes an acceptable risk, perhaps due to their youth and working-class background, and they will often tend to reject the advice and recommendations of their teachers.

What we see here is an almost classic description of conflict. One party is trying to persuade the other to change its behaviour, while the object of the persuasion does not see the necessity to do so. It is important to grasp that this conflict is based upon a clash of ideas, ideas about the appropriate attitude to death. Teachers get annoyed because their pupils do not appear to understand what is in their best interests, while pupils are perplexed at the teachers' failure to understand their point of view. To put the situation in the language of the philosophy of education, teachers appear to their pupils to be in authority on this topic, but not *an* authority (Peters, 1973). The pupils have to listen to them, and even pretend to agree with them, but they will find it difficult to be persuaded if their idea of an appropriate attitude to death is not shared by their teachers. There is a long history in British education of teachers trying to change the life-style of their pupils, whether in terms of what they eat, how they amuse themselves, what clothes they wear or what aspirations they have, and such attempts generally come up against the glass ceiling of a different attitude to life. Teachers and pupils are to all intents and purposes speaking a different language from each other, and the teachers are faced with the task of converting their pupils to a new way of life.

This description is potentially a rather worrying one. It suggests that there are strong structural reasons for expecting teachers and pupils to be unable to communicate across a whole range of important topics, in particular those relating to death and risk. What we are seeing here is a clash of values, and it is by no means self-evident that the values of teachers are preferable to those of their pupils. There is no objective standard of risk which specifies the limits of acceptable risk. It is for the individual to decide what sort of risk is acceptable, and provided that the individual has the relevant information, is not self-deceived and is not unduly coerced by the media or other powerful social forces, there should be no difficulty in assessing what sort of risk is involved. We shall see later on how this might be developed as an approach to personal and social education, but it needs to be emphasized that the teaching profession tends to undervalue the ability of pupils to make a reasonable judgement about risk since it is biased in favour of what it regards as reasonable in its own eyes. We have seen that a teacher's notion of reasonableness may well be a very different one from that adopted by his pupils. If any progress is to be possible here it is not going to lie in the development of ever more persuasive techniques to apply to pupils, but rather in teachers thinking about their own feelings about death and risk and how they might use those insights as a way of coming closer to an understanding of the attitudes of their pupils. This raises the possibility of a dialogue between pupils and teachers which could be highly productive both in general and especially for the mutual understanding of how different sorts of people think they ought to live.

CHAPTER 4

Talking to children about death

There are ways in which the curriculum encompasses the topic of death, and always has done. At all levels of schooling there exist contexts in which it is entirely natural to discuss death and related issues. It may be that the particular book which a class is reading deals with someone's death and its implications, or that a member of the class itself has died, or that a discussion springs up about a man-made or natural catastrophe. Children watch the news, and they are aware of world events, and their experience of the media is not limited to viewing death faked by actors. There is good reason to think that these opportunities for discussion are frequently not taken up by teachers, hesitant as they are to tackle this difficult subject and worried about what might happen if they do not get it right. One English teacher in a secondary school spoke of the distress and confusion he experienced when, while looking with his class at a novel by D. H. Lawrence in which a father dies, a girl burst into tears because of her memory of her own father's death. The description in the book had revived her grief, and she was unable to restrain herself from crying in public, something which obviously embarrassed her, but her teacher even more. Teachers often comment on the way the more 'emotional' members of a class could be quite easily upset by the use of such material, and even more by its subsequent discussion. As we have seen, there is a tendency to think that because pupils are young it is not really appropriate to introduce a subject like death into the classroom until they have reached a more mature stage of development.

There is also the very real problem of not really knowing how to treat such an important subject, a problem which particularly affects teachers because of their frequent inability to confront the concept of death themselves at a personal level. The desire to 'protect' pupils from negative experiences is less marked with older pupils, and yet it is present to a surprising degree. One might cynically wonder whether the teachers are concerned to protect the pupils or themselves, but it is no doubt prudent to worry about wandering into an area which is so imperfectly understood. Many teachers did admit that they do not really see that the topic of death is relevant to them as subject teachers, but regard it more as a matter for pastoral teachers or those concerned specifically with personal and social education (PSE). There is certainly something to be said for this view. Talking to young people who have been bereaved does call for special sensitivity and may well involve particular skills which it would be wrong to expect every teacher to possess. Yet from what we know of the mourning and bereavement experiences of young people it is very likely that the school has potentially a large contribution to make to a successful adjustment to loss.

Many of the young people I interviewed who had received some form of counselling were rather critical of the 'trouble-shooting' aspect of such contacts. As a 14-year-old girl in London whose mother had recently died commented:

> The counsellor kept on insisting that I talk about my feelings, and made me feel guilty if I didn't want to . . . She obviously had an idea of how I should be feeling, and what I should be doing, and I wasn't doing any of the right things, and so she wanted me to change. Typical of teachers, really . . . but I felt better just being left alone to sort myself out.

She later admitted that when she had worked out what the teacher wanted her to do and say she felt, she acted accordingly, and she watched with rather grim amusement the satisfaction creeping over the counsellor's face as she no doubt thought of the imminent closing of the file and a good job well done. Children often resent the way in which adults try to manipulate their feelings and the crudity with which this is sometimes done.

Some children who have received counselling felt that it was based upon a rather simplistic understanding of coping with loss and that it failed to pay much attention either to the individual situations of the children or to the variety of family reaction to loss. One 10-year-old girl whose older sister had been suddenly killed said that she felt that the teachers had put her in a special category as someone to whom they had to be exceptionally sympathetic. Yet she reported that:

> The best thing to happen in school was when one of the dinner ladies just put her arms around me and cried. She didn't even say what about, although we all knew, of course. I felt really good for a whole week after that.

A 13-year-old boy in London whose father had died was very critical of his teachers:

> The trouble with teachers is that they have a very simple idea about what you should be feeling and doing. I don't know how they know, since I don't know myself what I should feel, and it was *my* dad who died. They just want to poke their noses into everything you do. It's like when they talk about sex, they don't know what to say and they know they are being stupid in having to say something, however boring it is.

This is a typical response. Many pupils do not see teachers as the right people to discuss their loss with.

One might suspect that this is a reaction to teachers who do not know how to approach children suffering from a loss through death, but those teachers who have a background in counselling, or think they do, are often regarded as especially useless by their pupils, who preferred those who reacted as people and not as professionals. This is perhaps surprising, since one might expect that those teachers who have an understanding of the sorts of problems which may arise through the death of someone close to a pupil will be in a good position to help the pupil work through her feelings and cope with them. Sometimes this is done successfully, of course, but often pupils suspect that the teacher or counsellor expects a particular sort of reaction to loss from the pupil, and is not satisfied until he gets it. This is particularly true with teachers who are convinced that bereaved people must grieve properly if they are to avoid depression later on. This approach, which has been so well defended by Dora Black, stresses the importance of expressing one's grief. Bottling it up can lead to serious problems later, problems which it is difficult to address since they are so distant in time and place from the original bereavement which led to them. Teachers who are impressed with this theory tend to favour pupils who express their bereavement in a fairly explicit way, since it can then be seen that an appropriate form of bereavement has taken place, with the desirable consequence that it may well prevent the onset of mental illness later on. This theory seems highly plausible, but it can have an undesirable impact upon counselling practice, in that the counsellor may be so concerned to elicit the 'right' response that she does not notice that the individual with whom she is working is searching for a response which is right for him.

This is a point well worth emphasizing. One effect of the way death is treated in our society is to make the bereaved less sure of how they should behave. There is no longer a code of conduct which must be followed, except for those people who still live within a traditional structure of belief and community. For them there is a prescribed ritual which must be got through for the death to be properly marked. For most people, though, the ceremonies surrounding death are rather *ad hoc* and it can become very much a matter of individual choice what sort of ceremony is felt to be appropriate. At the time of the Hillsborough tragedy many Liverpudlians felt it was right to lay flowers and drape scarves at Anfield, and many of them said that this is what made them feel better. They had marked the deaths with a symbol of their grief, and that represented a stage in working through that grief. Yet there were many people who felt deeply sad about the tragedy and did not demonstrate their feelings physically in any direct way at all, and this was right for them. To think that less demonstrative behaviour is necessarily more damaging to the individual than the more demonstrative reactions of those who treated Anfield as a place of pilgrimage is surely too crude.

We tend to see grief as a process with stages, and the counsellor who is wedded to such a model mentally ticks off the stages while talking to the bereaved. This can be very useful, since for many people there are stages which can be clearly delineated and which have much the same status as the developmental stages in the psychological growth of a personality. It is very useful to be acquainted with the range of responses of bereaved people and to understand that their behaviour at a particular moment may signal an attempt, albeit confused, to move from one stage to another, with the ultimate end being an acceptance of the event and an ability to live with it. If we agree that death is something of a taboo in our society, and that religious allegiances are weak, there are grounds for being sceptical about the existence of a clearly definable process of grieving. As with so much of our behaviour, grief behaviour has to be learnt, and young people in particular may never have had an opportunity to observe such behaviour, so their ability to learn it is restricted. Counselling may well help them to release the emotions which they are bottling up inside, but it may also put pressure on them to display emotions which they do not wish to display, and which they can deal with in their own way. Bereaved children often react better to adults who feel with them rather than try to help them with professional detachment, since in many cases it is possible to communicate the feeling without any explicit display of emotion.

Let us give an example here. Julie was very friendly with another 13-year-old girl at her school in the West Midlands, and the latter was killed by a car while going home with Julie. Julie was obviously upset by this, and she spent a lot of time at school moping and not concentrating on her work or relationships with other children. She did not cry or even talk about the event. The school was concerned, and she spoke to a counsellor provided by the local education authority about it. She felt that the counsellor was concerned at her lack of open grief, and that the counsellor was pushing her, gently but firmly, into crying and talking at length about her feelings. Julie felt that she did not want to, and that it was appropriate for her to grieve for her friend in her own quiet way. When asked how her teachers had treated her after the accident she picked out as especially helpful her physical education teacher who:

> while discussing the preparations for a hockey match looked really sympathetic when she looked at me. She said nothing at all about the accident, or about Pam, the girl who was killed, and I thought she might, since Pam is normally in the team too. She realized that I did not want to talk about her, not then anyway, and she was happy to talk about ordinary things in a way which showed me that she was thinking of me and with me.

The teacher expressed her sympathy through her ordinary actions, as many people express their grief. She was sharing some of Julie's feelings, not trying to manipulate them, unlike the counsellor (on her interpretation). The teacher understood that she could show Julie that she was with her without doing anything out of the ordinary. It was the way she did it that Julie felt was important and indeed helpful.

Why do so many children find counsellors annoying? To a degree, it is because they identify them with teachers who, as adults, think they know what children ought to be feeling and doing and thus seek to impose some pattern of behaviour on them. Children are also well aware that the relationship they have with counsellors is a professional one, and that the counsellors expect to get results from the encounter. That is their purpose in being there, and children who are at least of secondary age understand this and can be rather suspicious of what is going on. Children's experience of formal education makes them very aware of adults' attempts to manipulate them. But, it will be said, children need helping, and the role of the counsellor is to help where children cannot help themselves. Children do not understand what is involved in bereavement and they have to be guided to react to bereavement in the right sort of way, otherwise they are in serious danger of suffering long-term psychological damage. As we have seen, society no longer provides clear rules about bereavement behaviour, and families may be ineffectual when faced within a child's need to grieve. So the child may become confused, introverted and isolated in her grief. This may lead to anxiety. The outward signs of this are anger and perhaps aggression, while inwardly she may feel distress and become withdrawn. In school this can result in poorer concentration, less commitment to work, inability to cooperate and a reduced capacity to conform.

If the child does not become actually disruptive in the classroom it can be easy not to notice the change in his behaviour. He will tend to withdraw from the activities of both the classroom and the playground. The academic side of his work may deteriorate rapidly, as can his ability to relate socially within the school. Unless the change in behaviour is very marked, teachers will find it difficult to spot, and unless they are aware of the situation which has led to the pupil's problems, they will not know how to explain any change in behaviour. The child may be going through a distressing and perplexing period of adjustment, and bereavement is a process during which a wide gamut of emotions will be experienced. The process is one of disbelief, belief, shock, distress, anger, rationalization, and finally acceptance. Some children will certainly require assistance to get through this process, and for some the final stage of acceptance will never be successfully attained. It is also true that many children do not understand that there is a pattern to the conflicting emotions which are part of bereavement, and they may require assistance in sorting out their ideas and fitting them into their lives. The period of schooling is, after all, a crucially important stage in their lives, when problems both academic and social can have far-reaching effects upon them and their future. Even a minor psychological problem resulting from bereavement can have major implications for the child's future, and it is important that help be available to get them through this difficult period of their lives.

It is difficult to know how effective such intervention is, though. Many children have undergone appropriate counselling and feel that it was not helpful. They could be mistaken, of course, and not appreciate how much it has helped them. Some children, perhaps, cannot be helped, but it is a fairly common complaint that counsellors try to hijack the emotions of their clients and take them somewhere they do not want to go. The counsellors think they know where those emotions ought to be, and they take steps to move them along, but the actual bearers of the emotions, the children themselves, do not in some cases feel in control of what is going on and they may become quite indignant at the way their approaches to bereavement are organized and pigeonholed by counsellors. Counsellors ought to be aware of this. Children can be quite passive and uncomplaining – this is after all a desideratum in most schooling – and as a result they may go along with the counsellor's suggestions, or pretend to do so, even though they are unconvinced that this is the right path to follow. The important point to make here is that the child should be in charge of her emotions in so far as this is feasible. What goes wrong with much of the bereavement process is that the child is no longer in control, since she is confused and at the mercy of conflicting emotions, and the role of the counsellor should be to help her regain control. This is unlikely to happen if the counsellor has an agenda which is different from that of the child. The child is then obliged to go along with the counsellor's ideas and loses her autonomy in the process. Not surprisingly, this will often lead to a lack of communication and failure to help the child.

It cannot be emphasized too strongly that children do not follow a single path to a successful bereavement. Children are different from each other, as are adults, and in our very diverse society they may feel the need to experience a form of bereavement which is appropriate for them. There is no useful point in insisting on a single route to the acceptance stage which lies at the end of bereavement, nor is it possible to find universal criteria for the attainment of this stage. Some children will come to terms with the situation very readily but not demonstrate their acceptance in the sorts of ways that counsellors expect. Others appear to have adapted to the loss in an appropriate manner, but in fact have not, and continue to have problems with it. Going through a bereavement experience is for children a very important developmental stage, a rite of passage almost, and they think it is more likely to be successful if it is a process which they operate. We have to be sensitive to the variety of forms of behaviour which children may exhibit on their route through this process, and this is something which we find difficult to do, since we tend to think that we as adults have a much better idea of what is going on than the people who are actually undergoing the process. We tend to lump children together to produce generalizations which allow us to group them together in intellectually satisfying ways, and as a result undervalue the differences which exist between them. This is particularly the case with teachers who have as their priority the teaching and controlling of a large group of children, and for whom a lengthy consideration of the personalities of the individuals in the class is a dangerous luxury.

CHAPTER 5

Talking to children about risk

One of the less obvious points about risk which I have already mentioned in this book is that attitudes towards it are conditioned by class differences. It is quite common to acknowledge a difference in attitude as a result of age, but it is important to realize that class is also a highly relevant factor. Working-class pupils will often see as acceptable a level of risk which middle-class pupils would reject, or at least treat as less acceptable. If the accounts of the socialization patterns of these two groups through schooling make any sense at all, then it is not implausible to expect to find differences in attitudes to risk here too. Since academic low-achievers might be seen as destined for occupations which involve little autonomy and relatively high levels of boredom and repetition, their leisure activities while young could compensate them for the tedium they experience at school. Implicit in the way they are treated in school – as incapable of taking sensible and valid decisions – is a lack of confidence in their ability to structure their leisure profitably. More academic pupils, by contrast, will be treated by teachers as more adult and responsible individuals, and they will be trusted to resolve situations in relatively mature and acceptable ways. This may make them adopt a rather different attitude to their leisure activities, so that they assess what the implications of a particular lifestyle are for them, rather than waiting to see what the consequences turn out to be.

This is possibly an over-simplification, but the interviews which have been reproduced here suggest that attitudes to risk among young people are significantly linked to their social origins and to the way they are regarded at school. Pupils who are treated by their teachers as unlikely to make sensible decisions could easily grow up into adults who find it harder to make what might be regarded as sensible decisions. As we have seen, what often happens in the confrontation between teachers and pupils is that there is a culture clash, with teachers, who are predominantly middle-class and older, trying to foist their ideas on to younger, working-class pupils. The teacher tries to get the pupil to see what is wrong with the pupil's attitude to risk, and is surprised when the pupil resists. In just the same way that pupils tend to resist forms of academic schooling which they regard as alien and inimical to their interests, so they may also resist the way schooling tries to impose upon them an attitude to risk, and indeed to life in general, which involves a challenge to their ideas of themselves and of their likely futures. This is by no means a problem limited to attitudes to risk, but can be widened to include attitudes to work, domestic responsibilities and leisure opportunities. For example, teachers may try to persuade pupils that they should consider avenues of work which run against the sex stereotypes prevalent in their community, and from what might be regarded as an objective point of view there is a lot to be said for such a suggestion. While many pupils might find such work interesting and worthwhile, it is far from easy to go against the ideas of friends and family when deciding what work one is to undertake. This is especially the case if the arguments for taking that decision are provided by teachers who have throughout one's school career been seen as advocates of forms of knowledge and ways of working which are profoundly strange to the view of the world of many of their pupils.

Let me give an example. I remember listening to a teacher telling his pupils about the benefits to be derived from trying out an activity which initially seems strange and unattractive. He had for some months been spending his weekends digging out canals in Wales, as part of a conservation project. He was telling his pupils, in this case 14-year-olds in a Greater Manchester secondary school, what he enjoyed about the activity and what he liked about canals. Clearly his description of the activity interested the pupils, but they were amazed that he was prepared to do it for nothing, and they found it difficult to understand what it was he liked about canals. When he went on at some length about the beauty of the Victorian canals, I saw many pupils exchange glances, as though to acknowledge the eccentricity of this enthusiasm. One of the interesting things which came out of the discussion that ensued was that the canal work was rather risky, a point which they were happy to make when he started to talk about the dangers of smoking! They cleverly got him to extend his discussion of the delights of canals, pretending to be interested but really they were amazed that anyone could find such places worth examining in detail, and working hard to restore. What is interesting about this situation is that we have here a teacher who is of a similar background to his pupils, who comes from the same part of the country and who is not very much older than they are in absolute terms, who even lives in the same neighbourhood as his pupils, yet there is a large gap between the experiences and attitudes of the parties involved. They just cannot see what it is that interests him about canals, and he cannot see what does not interest them about canals. The longer the discussion goes on, the wider the gulf grows.

What happens when this same teacher talks to the class about risk? They associate what he has to say about risk with what he has already said about his leisure interests, and so are rather dismissive about it. The point here is not that unpopular teachers are unlikely to be very successful in changing the attitudes of pupils, although this is probably true. The teacher in the example I have just given was popular, and an effective and skilful communicator. But the pupils found his views on risk just as difficult to take seriously as his leisure activities. They needed something concrete they could identify with in this teacher, in order to be able to take on board his views on, in this case, smoking, and all they could find was someone with eccentric and pointless (and profitless) ways of spending his spare time. He was hardly in a position to influence them as far as smoking was concerned, since they did not feel he was enough like them. Although they could appreciate the logic of his arguments against smoking, on an emotional level they could not relate those arguments to themselves.

Middle-class teachers of working-class pupils often regard themselves as rather like the missionaries who went out to 'primitive' tribes to convert them to Christianity and bring them the benefits of civilization. Teachers feel they know what is in the interests of their pupils, and if pupils would only understand what their interests are, they would greatly benefit. Teachers know that if pupils work hard, do well in their examinations and look after their health, then they will grow up to be useful and fit members of society; it is their job as teachers, they feel, to tell them this. They are in a similar position to their Victorian predecessors, setting out to convert the heathen. This attitude is unlikely to be effective in contemporary society, though, and only the most charismatic teachers are going to have any prospect of success. Many teachers will encounter resistance to what they are trying to do: pupils will reject their arguments about risk just as much as they reject the arguments which are to be found in the academic curriculum. This resistance and rejection is not so much directed at the content, but more at the context. Pupils may respect their teachers, but they may find it difficult to identify with them. Many schools are very hierarchic institutions, and it is perhaps inevitable that those at the bottom of the hierarchy will find it difficult to identify with those at the top. In some schools there is not much difference between the class basis of teachers and pupils which can lead to such identification becoming easier, and some of the interviews bear this out. Yet in many schools there are yawning chasms between staff and pupils, and such chasms can be difficult to bridge.

When a teacher talks to her pupils about risk, she has to accomplish a number of things. First of all, she has to convince them of the validity of her argument. Then she has to get them to see how they should relate that argument to their lives, since if all that happens is that they accept it intellectually, it is hardly likely to change their behaviour. A teacher's expertise lies in his ability to manipulate and explain facts and theories, not in his power to persuade pupils to adopt or avoid particular lifestyles. The current government is keen that teachers should take on this more admonitory role, but there is little evidence that they would be much good at it. Perhaps this is because teachers do not actually know any better than pupils what attitudes should be held towards risk, since this is essentially a moral and personal issue which the individual has to work towards on his or her own.

Surely this is not right, though. The teacher might be expected to have the advantage not only of more knowledge than the pupil, but also of a greater weight of experience which she can share with the pupil, enabling him to decide in a more rational manner what is to be done. But is this really true? Consider this conversation which I recorded in a Midlands school. The young female teacher was giving a PSE lesson and was talking about the dangers of smoking. She knew that many of the teenage girls in the school were quite heavy smokers, and she wanted to persuade them that this was a risky activity, since it is likely to harm them physically, and also damage any children they might have later. She provided the pupils with a variety of what I thought were well-organized lessons in which the facts relating to smoking were clearly and even dramatically illustrated, and then she asked the pupils what effect they thought this might have on their present and future behaviour. One 16-year-old girl responded:

> Well, we know all that, Miss, but can't we do what we like with our bodies? I mean, if we know what the risks are, why can't we just take them? I watch you cycle into school every day, and you are on that rickety bike wobbling all over the place between all those lorries, breathing in all those fumes and just missing being knocked over. What's so risky about smoking in comparison?

When the teacher was asked about her leisure activities, it emerged that one of these was rock-climbing, and the pupils suggested quite plausibly that this was also quite a risky activity (this had been a week in which several climbing fatalities had been widely reported), and the implication was that if it is all right for the teacher to take risks, then it is just as acceptable for pupils to do the same, albeit in different ways. The teacher in this case found it difficult to respond effectively to her pupils. She pointed out that while there was risk attendant on her activities, the activities themselves were likely to prolong rather than endanger health, but this explanation was given short shrift. As a boy suggested:

> The thing is, we know that smoking is dangerous, but we don't know anyone who is ill through smoking, or who has died. We do have mates who have been knocked down by cars, and when you think about it, just one swerve of the bike will bring you right up against a car, and that will be your lot. Just one careless or sleepy driver who doesn't see you is enough to kill you. You have to smoke a lot of cigarettes for a long time before they might harm you, and my nan has been smoking all her life, she never has a fag out of her mouth, and she has been going for a long time, and she's pretty healthy, there's nothing wrong with her.

The teacher felt frustrated at the way the discussion had gone. She was looking for something she could produce which would convince the pupils of the excessively risky nature of smoking, and even those pupils who did not smoke were thoroughly unmoved by her arguments and refused to go where those arguments were supposed to take them.

Was the teacher doing anything wrong? She had constructed an interesting lesson, and it was clearly one in a series which had succeeded in provoking the pupils to talk, and this was certainly an aim she set herself. But she was thoroughly dissatisfied with the direction the conversation had taken. She wanted to change the behaviour of her pupils, open their eyes to the harm they were doing to themselves, and yet even those pupils who were not engaged in the activity in question were unconvinced by her approach. What quite clearly emerged in the discussion was that many of the pupils saw the teacher trying to impose on them a view of the world and their part in it which is both alien and arbitrary. It is arbitrary because the teacher was seen to be applying double standards, advocating the avoidance of only certain sorts of risk, not the sorts of risk which applied to her own activities and interests. It is alien because the teacher's activities are quite distinct from those which the pupils would consider undertaking. They did cycle to school, but had they been old enough and wealthy enough to drive, they thought they certainly would. Anyone who earns a salary and who chooses to risk the vagaries of the weather and the busy road to cycle to school is exhibiting a strange and somewhat inexplicable lifestyle. They found it difficult to understand why she behaved in that way, and she found it difficult to understand why they behave the way they do, since from her point of view she was engaging in healthy activities which have a degree of risk, but an acceptable degree of risk.

What was unsatisfactory in this confrontation between teacher and pupils is precisely that it did turn into a confrontation, and not a conversation. In a genuine conversation there is dialogue. Both parties are prepared to listen to the other and to be affected by what they hear. Now, pupils are often happy to accept what they hear from teachers – after all, they know that they are younger and less well-educated than their teachers, so the latter may have some useful information to impart. Yet many pupils are capable of making quite a sharp distinction between those areas of knowledge where teachers really have some degree of expertise, and those areas where they do not. Teachers are trained to teach a particular subject or field of study, and they are obviously presumed to know far more about it than their pupils. Outside of this quite narrow area, though, is there any reason why pupils should listen respectfully to their teachers? Do the latter know any more than their pupils about moral and political issues, for instance, or about how to organize one's life? Certainly teachers are older, and have access to greater reserves of experience, yet this does not necessarily make them experts on morality or politics, or indeed on anything else where values are relevant. It might be hoped that teachers are capable of producing a structure within which value issues can be raised and discussed in a reasonably impartial and productive manner, but the actual views of teachers themselves have no privileged status compared with the views of their pupils.

It is important to make this distinction between those aspects of the curriculum which are justifiably led by teachers and those to which teachers can make a contribution, but no more. Of course, it might be argued that throughout the curriculum teachers should not seek to set themselves up as experts, but should try to guide pupils to work out the answers for themselves, using teachers as a resource to be consulted rather than as an oracle to be obeyed. There are many contexts in which such an approach constitutes a positive teaching strategy, and encourages the autonomy and independence of the pupil. Yet it should be readily acknowledged that the teacher knows more about the topic than the pupil, and in so far as the teacher is preparing pupils for examinations, she is giving precise instructions on how to present their work and ideas in ways which will accord with the expectations of the examiners. In the language of the philosophy of education, the teacher is *in* authority through being *an* authority; the pupils follow her suggestions because they appreciate that she knows what she is talking about, and it is to their advantage to listen to her. But there are many topics on which the teacher may be in authority, but certainly not an authority. Are teachers likely to have any greater insight as to how people ought to live than anyone else? Anyone acquainted with the sort of individuals who inhabit staffrooms would find that difficult to accept. Teachers are no more likely to be ethically sound than their pupils, or anyone else, and they are no more likely to organize their lives efficiently or to avoid risk than people in other walks of life. While pupils may genuinely like and respect their teachers, they will often be quite capable of distinguishing between the questions to which the teachers have the solutions, and those questions to which they have no privileged access at all.

Teachers spend so much of their professional (and sometimes private) lives telling people what to do that it is difficult for them to put themselves in the position of not knowing how to act. They may well be so used to regarding themselves as the fount of knowledge on a particular subject area that they come to regard themselves as an authority on a wide variety of topics and subjects. It is evident that if one spends a great deal of one's time being in charge, in a position of authority, it is not always easy to take up a different position, to listen to the comments of others and treat them as worthy of consideration. Teachers may not be sufficiently sensitive to the distinction between the topics on which they are authorities and those on which they are not. It is, after all, quite natural to expect to be listened to with a degree of acquiescence whatever one is talking about if, as a teacher, one spends most of the time speaking quite positively and aggressively to pupils. Yet it is by no means difficult for children to tell when a teacher knows what she is talking about, and when she is just expressing her personal opinions. The present government would be well-advised to take note of this. It would not then insist that teachers seek to reinforce conventional morality as part of the traditional curriculum as though it were just another subject which could be taught. It can indeed be taught, but not in the same way as the subjects in the National Curriculum.

One area where the teacher can do no more than give her point of view is when she talks about risk. The teacher is presenting her ideas about risk, and is backing up those ideas with an appropriate description of the facts. What should ideally take place is that teachers and pupils come to understand and respect each other's views. Discussing risk is an excellent opportunity for this to take place, since there is a lot of scope here for a genuine sharing of ideas. From the teacher's point of view, it is important that children consider all the implications of their actions, and face clearly the nature of what they intend doing. This is not a simple task to accomplish. For example, suppose that a pupil is prepared to smoke despite the risks. He must be able to understand what those risks are if his decision is to be reasonable. Now, someone might say that there is no way in which such a decision could be reasonable, since this is an activity which has no obvious advantages and many serious disadvantages. It is also an activity which is addictive, so that once the individual starts, he is going to find it increasingly difficult to change his mind. Even before he has started to smoke, one might question what influences the pupil has quite unconsciously internalized, ranging from peer pressure to advertising, and this also raises the issue of how free he is to make such a decision. This is true, though, of a whole range of activities, even those for which it is easier to find a rationale. Physical exercise can also be addictive, and one may undertake it through peer and advertising pressure. The important point about discussions of risk is that the individual has to be able to represent to himself the likely consequences of his actions in a way which is more than just intellectual. He has to be able to imagine what it would be like for the negative consequences of the activity to take place, and how it would affect him, and indeed others connected with him.

Some risks are hardly worth considering. While I am sitting at my desk typing this page out there is no doubt a risk that an aeroplane which is approaching the nearby airport will crash on to my house, so that the safest place I could be is in the basement or somewhere else entirely. Yet if I rushed to the door every time I heard an aeroplane overhead I should rightly be judged over-anxious, unless perhaps there was something in my history which made such a concern more than neurotic. But many risks are worth thinking about, especially when they involve either our lives or wellbeing in a serious way. Teachers are good at talking about the factual basis of risk assessment and they have a lot of experience of discussing the ways in which risk is involved in many of the activities we wish to pursue. Of course, this relates to that part of the curriculum which is based on knowledge. Teachers may understand precisely why particular activities are far more dangerous than they initially seem since they know more about those activities than pupils. Even though they may not have actually taken part in these activities, they have a better understanding of what they constitute than the relatively ignorant pupils whose point of view on those activities may well be more limited than is desirable. It would be difficult to deny that teachers have an important contribution to make to the general discussion in school of the acceptability of particular ways of life and their associated practices.

Where teachers have less of a contribution to make is in assessing the nature and importance of the risk. For many people, and especially for many young people, the risk connected to an activity is what gives that activity its flavour and interest. Why does young drivers' insurance cost more? Because insurance companies know that young people are likely to be more reckless drivers, and this is not necessarily because they have less driving experience. They enjoy driving fast, taking risks to impress others with the verve of their driving and not keeping closely to the traffic regulations. This is part of what makes the activity of driving enjoyable for them. Since they are likely to have less experience of the dangers of driving, they will give those dangers less weight than older drivers. Now, teachers can certainly talk about this latter aspect of reckless driving. They can point out what happens when accidents occur and what it looks like to be involved in such accidents, but they cannot do much to affect the desirability of a fairly casual attitude to the rules of driving. The risk is part of the attraction, and to criticize that attitude is to attempt to encourage young people to adopt more middle-aged attitudes to risk, a project which is unlikely to be successful.

What is more likely to succeed is a frank admission on the part of teachers that there is no objective way risk can be assessed in such cases. This would then enable them to discuss such activities with their pupils, rather than laying down the law as to how those activities should be regarded. For example, a teacher might accept that different people have different attitudes to risk, and also that it is worthwhile to discuss and examine those differences. The teacher may say that she is very concerned about preserving her health, and will avoid those activities which are likely to harm her health, because she values her health very highly. She is prepared to think quite carefully about it before she changes her behaviour, and she has a firm image of the sort of person she wants to be. This is a person who is in control of herself physically, as far as this is possible given the vagaries of human life. She is presenting a model of how she wants her life to be, and she is prepared to tell the children that this is what she wants for herself. This also serves to put the lifestyle she has chosen into a useful context. Suppose she is confronted with a child who has a different idea how to live, an idea which does not place such a premium on health. Both parties are then in a good position to help each other understand what it is about their contrasting lifestyles which they find attractive, and this is at least one step on the road to mutual comprehension.

To illustrate this, it is interesting to examine the following conversation between a male primary school teacher and his class of 8-year-olds in Merseyside. The teacher had been very worried about the children's proclivity, especially that of the boys, to play on the railway lines near their homes. The underground system ran in the area, and it was not difficult for the children to climb over or between the railings onto the track. It was not uncommon for children to do this in order to amuse themselves, and the railway line obviously represented for them an exciting and challenging area for recreation. The teacher started off by talking about the dangers of playing anywhere near the lines, and explained that not only was there a danger of collision with the trains but that the electricity cables were also potentially lethal. He realized while he was going through these facts with the children that they knew all this very well, but that it was not for them a reason to avoid the activity. On the contrary, it provided a reason to continue with it. Here are some of the children's replies.

I love playing down there ... it's very private, with all the prickly bushes and that, and you find stuff down there, and it's good fun to chase the rats with bits of sticks you pick up and that. When the busies come and chase you they've got no chance to catch you, they hate hurting themselves on the prickles and they can't find us in the holes down there, and they haven't got the nerve to cross the lines, but we do.

Teacher: But isn't it dangerous? Do you remember John before Christmas who was killed down there, and Mark who fell off that pole and hurt his back? Wouldn't it be better to play somewhere safer?

Yeah, well it can be a bit rough down there, but that's what I like about it. You've got to be tough to stick it, it's no good being soft. It's not for girls (*lots of jeering at this stage*). You can get hurt, if you're unlucky, if you're a divvie, like. That's what Mark was, he was stupid to get up there and swing around, I wouldn't try that. But it's great to lark around a bit, have a bit of a run, be a bit of a nutter, it's sound.

When I get down there, you're like in a world by yourself. I mean, it's quiet, no one knows you're there, you can do what you like, you can roll a log down the slope onto the trains if you like, no one can stop you, and you just sit there and watch the trains and think that they don't know you're there, they think they're all right but they're only all right if we don't do, like, anything on the rails. When the trains aren't there it's dead quiet, you can hear the birds, watch the bunnies ...

At the end of the discussion the teacher felt rather defeated. He wanted to present the children with strong arguments against wandering round the railway, and they seemed to be more successful in presenting arguments in support of their behaviour.

There is a tendency for teachers in this sort of situation to throw their hands up in the air (metaphorically or otherwise) and give up. After all, if pupils reject their urgings on these topics, then they only have those rejections to blame when they eventually suffer the consequences of their actions. Once one has done everything which can be done to dissuade, nothing more can be done. Indeed, the more one persists in raising the issue, the more attractive it may seem to some of the children, since they quickly come to realize that the teacher is quite shocked by some of the things they do. The primary teacher in my example thought about the response of the children in his class and refused to give up. He understood that the most efficient approach was not to reject out of hand what the children were saying, but to try to grasp their point of view and work out how to make his worries about their behaviour more real to them. He appreciated that they had already been told on many other occasions by their parents, police and the railway staff that they should not do what they were doing, that it is dangerous and harmful to others as well as to themselves, and that there was little point his adding his comments to the familiar refrain. What is required is a way of putting his view which is likely to strike a chord in the children.

So instead of haranguing the children, he started to get them to talk about what they liked about playing round the track. As we have seen from some of the children's comments, they could wax quite lyrical about the natural delights of that area, and when the teacher went to inspect it himself he was impressed by the natural terrain, the wildness of the environment and the large number of animals which inhabited the space. It made a potent contrast with the bleak urban landscape of the immediate area. It was quite clear that one of the aspects of the spot they valued was quite acceptable – that is, its natural features. The desire to be away from other people is quite comprehensible, too, although less desirable from a safety point of view. What was particularly objectionable about the activities of the children was their potential danger both for themselves and for others. It was not uncommon for children to try to derail trains, and even for shots and other missiles to be directed at drivers and passengers. On top of this, many children over the years had been injured or even occasionally killed. It has also to be said that a number of other undesirable activities went on in this area in connection with substance abuse and fighting, so all in all this sort of area is a highly inappropriate playground for young children. Yet it became obvious during the discussion with the teacher that the children were not unaware of this. They knew about the dangers which lurked there, and that was one of its big attractions for them. They enjoyed participating in the dangerous activities, and the more dangerous these were the more motivated they were to get involved.

The teacher thought that the best way to proceed was to try to get the children to think about what the consequences of their behaviour might be. This involved talking about what happens when people are maimed or killed. He got some interesting answers to the question as to what happens when someone gets burnt on something carrying a high electricity current:

> Well, they just go black, and jerk about a bit, and smoke comes out of their ears. There's a flash and your clothes sort of burn. You could be killed, or just burnt. Your face is twisted-up after, like, and there's this horrible smell . . .

So it is clear that many of the children had a good idea of what might happen to them, since this description produced by one child was echoed by many others, who could often give examples from practical experience. The teacher was quite shocked at the assumed bravado of the boys in particular recounting these details, but he managed not to show it too strongly, and he went on talking to them about it. One thing was clear: the children had indeed thought about the consequences of their actions, and they had even pictured what it would be like were it to happen to them. These were not individuals who were acting with little or no thought as to the possible outcome of their behaviour. On the contrary, they knew from personal experience what could easily happen and most of them had thought about what it would be like were it to happen to them. What they had not really thought about was what it would mean to suffer the consequences in a long-term sense, what they would be missing were they to be killed or injured. They concentrated upon the physical results of things going wrong, but only had a vague idea of the consequences of those physical results. It seemed likely to me that their descriptions of what could happen, accurate though they were, borrowed quite heavily from some of the more gruesome videos which were obviously circulating in their homes.

This shows the contrast between more adult views of injury and those more common with children. The latter concentrate upon the short-term and dramatic aspects of disaster, while the former have a clear idea of what it may mean in the long term. The teacher knew that there were many things which he would like to continue to do, and premature death and injury would prevent that stream of future possibilities from being realized. The children had no such well-developed view of the future, which seemed to them to be a very vague and shadowy notion. What interested them most about things going wrong was precisely the events, not their consequences. The teacher then tried to explore some of the future paths which would inevitably be blocked off by things going wrong. He started by asking the children what they wanted to do in the future, and when he did not get much of a response, he encouraged them to think about and develop their concept of the future by writing, drawing and talking about it. In this particular class the girls had a much more defined notion of the future, at least initially, and it took some time for the boys to commit themselves.

One of the boys, John, who spent a lot of time around the railway, moved from saying this:

> I don't know, haven't thought about it really. I fancy being a pilot, I suppose ... flying, getting lots of money, going to work ...

to this:

> I'd like to join the army. They do lots of things, and you get to be with your mates all the time, and the money is good, and you go off to different places, swimming and boating and that, and climbing if you want to. I want to drive a tank and go dead fast through lots of mud, and if anyone gets in the way, turn the gun on the top on him and say, 'Get out of my way or you're going to get it'.

John was able to talk a lot about what he thought the army would be like, what it would require him to do and what he would enjoy and not enjoy about it. He was able to write about it and draw pictures of himself in a tank with a rifle. Initially, though, he had no idea of what a pilot did, could not draw himself in an aeroplane and had no conception of what might be involved. When he spoke about being a pilot he could not develop his ideas at all, and just repeated the same phrases in the way children talk when they are not interested in what they are saying and are just going through the motions under pressure from their teacher. It was quite clear at the beginning that John had no idea at all about a future as an adult, and he did not even show much interest in his future as an older child, which seemed very hazy to him. The teacher spent time getting him to work out some ideas here too, so that by the end of the periods of discussion John had worked out that it might be fun to go to a particular school, to future football matches and to get certain presents for the birthdays and holidays which stretched in front of him.

Now, it would certainly be wrong to think that once John had developed these more complex ideas about his future, he would think twice before indulging in his previous risky behaviour. What had been achieved was that John was now in a better position to see why the teacher was so worried about that behaviour, and he could understand why adults were interested in trying to change his behaviour. A similar point could be made about the people in trains whose wellbeing was threatened by the actions of the boys. Once they were seen as real people with possible futures of their own, it became easier to see why those futures are worth preserving. It was much easier to take a casual attitude to the people in trains when they were seen as just shapes at the window, but once they were seen as people, like the boys themselves, they could be regarded as having interests worth safeguarding. Had the teacher just harangued the children with the principle that it is wrong to harm innocent people, he would have been listened to but his words would have had little impact. Once he had undertaken to show what it was about them which made them worthy of respect, he was well on the way to making the children consider their interests. It is interesting how during these discussions the characterization of the people in the trains changed, for whereas initially they were drawn very crudely and sparingly, as in Figure 5.1, later on they were presented in much more detail as in Figure 5.2, and when the children wrote about them they were able to add far more in the way of description than was possible initially. The teacher encouraged the children to develop stories about the passengers and drivers. To start off with, these were brief and really rather two-dimensional. It was difficult for many of the children to regard them as more than just shapes to be glimpsed from the railway verge. Later on, though, the children gave them histories, and were capable of both talking and writing at some length about them.

It would be nice to be able to say that once the children were able to see not only their own futures but also the futures of others in three dimensions, as important realities, then they started to change their attitudes to what they were doing. But it would be wrong. There is no reason to think that being able to take a deeper view of these topics need alter the behaviour of anyone in any way at all. On the other hand, it does give children more of a context within which to make more informed decisions. The teacher is not telling the children what they ought to do, or how they should behave. He is not offering his view of the world as the approach they should follow. He is on the contrary opening up a dialogue with them, presenting his view as an alternative to their view, but not just an alternative, more of a development of their

Figure 5.1

Figure 5.2

view. He is suggesting that their view leaves out a lot of interesting material which extends what they know into more complete forms of knowledge. We need to stress the description of this process as being 'interesting'. What we see here is children using their imagination to add depth and breadth to their view of the world, a process which enables them to colour in the moral background that had previously been only roughly sketched out. The teacher is genuinely working with the children to discover what their approach to the world is, and he is pointing to ways in which they can supplement that approach with additional and relevant information. He is not telling them that they are wrong and he is right.

It might be argued that this is something of an evasion. Surely the teacher is concerned to impress upon children that certain moral norms are important, and that the sorts of behaviour which attract them are just wrong. There is no doubt that teachers have firm moral beliefs and that they seek to convey these beliefs to their pupils, and there is nothing wrong with this. It is part of the role of teachers to help socialize children into the moral system of our society, for prudential as well as ethical reasons. My argument is that they are far more likely to be effective if they go about such moral persuasion by seeking to open up a genuine conversation with their pupils, a dialogue in which both parties learn a lot about each other. Thinking about death and loss is an obvious way in which this can be done, for there are no experts in attitudes to death. The teacher knows no more about how one should regard or approach death than his pupils. There is no objective standard of risk which demands a generally acceptable attitude towards it. Teachers have to work out what their response is going to be in just the same way as their pupils, and there is genuine pedagogical merit in being open about this.

CHAPTER 6

Disasters and ordinary tragedies

Disasters can make a dramatic impact upon the lives of survivors. It is the incidence of disasters which makes people wonder, often for the first time, how to explain to children what has happened. Disasters can be international, national or restricted to a relatively small locality but what they have in common is that the event is given some public status as of exceptional significance. There is a big difference between the numerous individual deaths of people on our roads and the death of an equivalent number where this happens all at once in a single accident, such as a motorway pile-up or a bus crash. Similarly, every year individual sailors perish at sea while fishing, but there is a difference between such individual events and the occurrence of a major event such as the sinking of one particular boat with the loss of many lives. Disasters highlight the fact that life is a purely temporary event, which can be brought to an end at any time, and the intensive coverage the media employ on such occasions tends to dramatize this fact. Different sorts of media use different methods of relating the disaster, with the more popular media emphasizing the personal while the more 'serious' media concentrate upon the technical aspects of the event. As I argued when looking at the ways social class affects attitudes and expectations, there is a tendency for the middle class to seek to grasp the meaning of the event in a different way from the working class. Working-class people are closer to death and disability, and they are interested in looking at different ways of coping with it, while middle-class observers seek to preserve their distance from the emotional consequences of the event by concentrating upon the precise pattern of causality which brought it about.

There is also something of a gender distinction in reactions to death. Women tend to feel able to express their emotions more freely, while men may not. Men will often seek to sublimate their feelings, either through practical work to raise money to help survivors, or by publicizing the dangers of the activities which led to the death, or by contributing to the relief of the suffering caused by such events. In our society women are brought up to be more expressive and to allow their emotions to develop more freely than men who are expected to be tougher and more resilient. For example, when I asked girls how they reacted to the death of someone close to them, they were not worried about admitting that they had cried, and that they had spent time with other girls mourning the loss in quite overt ways. Boys, on the other hand, were less likely to admit to such behaviour, and they were dubious about its acceptability. For example, I interviewed children in a school in the Home Counties which had suffered the deaths of a number of children in a minibus accident. A fairly representative reaction was provided by this 13-year-old girl:

> We were shocked by what happened, and when we came into school we just got together and cried and cried. The teachers tried not to, but I could see that they wanted to really. After a bit we sort of forgot about it, and got on with our normal work, but in the breaks we got together again and just talked about our friends, and then we cried again. When we got back to the classroom and looked at the empty desks we could not stop crying. It was not until the end of the week that we stopped, but we still think about them, what they should be doing with us now . . . I still sometimes feel upset about it, and when I saw the mum of one of the girls we cried again (this was three months after the event).

Far fewer boys had expressed themselves in this way, although some had, but for a briefer period. One 13-year-old boy, who had been quite friendly with two of the victims said:

> When we came into school the next day, it really hit us that they were not coming back. I think until then it was all sort of unreal, but when they weren't there, then I realized what it meant. I felt like crying, but although lots of the girls did, I didn't, none of the boys did. We felt sad about it, and talked about it a bit, but there is no point in going on about it, is there? I mean, it won't bring them back. You've just to get on with things, haven't you? All this crying is a bit of a waste of time.

When I asked this boy what he would think about boys who cried as the girls had done, he said that it would not have been right. It would not be appropriate male behaviour.

It is hardly surprising that there are distinctions between the mourning behaviour of boys and girls. Boys and girls are socialized differently in our society: boys are generally expected to be tougher both physically and mentally than girls, and they are expected to put up with more pain without expressing their feelings than girls. This 'macho' image is still important for a lot of boys, and it involves being less inclined to be frank about one's emotional life. It hardly fits in with the more aggressive aspects of the image to reveal one's feelings, and it is certainly suspect to admit that one is not in control of those feelings. Now, it is of course true that the stereotype of the tough boy and the gentle girl is often not an accurate indication of how girls and boys grow up in our society, and there are plenty of instances in which the crude stereotype is modified or even transposed. As the roles of men and women change in our society, no doubt it will become more acceptable for women to be less concerned with their feelings and more acceptable for men to think of themselves as caring and nurturing people, and this will have implications for their reactions to death and loss. But at the moment it is by no means difficult to argue that men and women, and boys and girls, take up quite different approaches to this area of social life.

Let us examine some of the reactions to what I am quite loosely calling disasters here. Children who are bereaved as a result of these events may react in a wide variety of ways. They may have been caught up in the disaster itself and so have witnessed scenes of death and injury, probably for the first time in their lives. They may have been unharmed and even helped with the injured. They may not have been anywhere near the event, but have come to hear about it through their school or the media. There is quite a common sequence of feelings which occurs in these cases. First of all, there is relief that one had survived. Many of the children I interviewed spoke of this, and it clearly made them feel rather guilty. They could so easily have been in the position of the victims, perhaps they were even supposed to have been with the victims but had to do something else instead, and the very first emotion they experience when they hear the news is that they were lucky. A phrase which cropped up again and again was 'It could have been me.' Actually, it is in itself an interesting fact that so many children should experience feelings of relief when someone close to them perishes, which is akin to the 'survivor syndrome' experienced by many members of the armed forces during a war. The survivor feels a temporary elation that someone else has suffered in the place, as it were, of the survivor. This is a feeling which quite naturally leads to subsequent, or even immediate, feelings of guilt, since it is obvious to the survivor that that elation is morally suspect. The survivor should be feeling sad at the death, and yet may not do so at the beginning. Quite a few of the children, especially the girls, wondered to what extent they were crying for their friends, and how much for themselves out of relief that they were still around to feel anything at all.

Counsellors may descend on a school to assist the children with their feelings, but, as we have seen, much of this 'help' is of dubious benefit. In any case, it is generally quite temporary in nature, since after a while they go away again, and such counsellors are not the natural people to whom children go for support. The obvious source of help is going to be friends, relatives and GPs. While these groups are initially going to be interested in the feelings of the disaster victims, as we may call the bereaved children, after a while they become more detached, and it is not usually long before they start suggesting that it is time to 'pull yourself together' and stop raking over the past. This is particularly prevalent when the bereaved person has no physical injuries as a result of the disaster. She may manifest behaviour which is rather strange and which the observer can relate to the disaster, but this is not necessarily the case, since the bereaved person may quite successfully cloak her problems within quite normal behaviour. Even if her behaviour becomes rather strange, the normal run of people to whom she can turn will often not have the skills either to understand what she is going through or to work out what to do about it. Since we live in a society which does not make much of a fuss about death, it is difficult to know what to do about an individual whose behaviour provides evidence of just such a fuss being made. Since bereaved people are expected to get back to normality after quite a short period, we do not really have the vocabulary to deal with those who are unwilling or unable to conform to our expectations.

Adults are not being callous when they urge children to pull themselves together. They are just reflecting the rather distant attitude which society has towards death. This is especially strong in the case of bereaved children, of whom it is frequently said that they have their whole lives ahead of them, and so they should regard the disaster as just a regrettable stage in that life, something which can justifiably hold up their progress for a while, but which should not be allowed to be a protracted obstacle to their development into adulthood. This is quite true, of course. A bereavement should not completely overturn the life of the individual, and we may hope that the many pleasant experiences which will take place in the future lives of people who are now young will serve to compensate for at least some of their negative experiences. Yet many young people require more time and space in which to recover their sense of themselves and where they are going than is provided by those adults and friends to whom they would normally go for support. This need not result in post-traumatic stress disorder, nor in the chronic grief, physical problems or mental instability which may occur, yet it seems likely that these serious consequences of disasters are closely linked with an environment in which the young person has reduced opportunity to achieve a satisfactory resolution of her feelings about the bereavement.

Children do often change as a result of their bereavement, and their friends notice those changes. When a disaster takes place, all the children involved in the bereavement may undergo changes of one sort or another, and this can bring about a very different atmosphere in a school or in a family. What many children say is that they felt very much better if they were all in the same boat, as it were. With a national disaster it is not difficult to put what has happened within some sort of broader context. It is featured on the television news and much discussed both on television and in newspapers. Specialists may come to the school to talk about it and offer help. In assembly the head discusses it, and offers to support children who are having problems in coming to terms with the situation. The children themselves are drawn together by the event, and traditional hostilities are restrained as new friendships are created. While children may feel guilty at their elation at being survivors, the elation itself may be a very pleasant feeling and may persist for a long time. Referring to the Hillsborough disaster, one 11-year-old boy who had lost his best friend admitted:

> When I got up to go to school a few days afterwards it was a really nice day, and I got a packet of sweets on the way to school, and I

thought to myself, 'Well, Pete is missing this, and I'm sorry about that, but isn't it great to be able to do it.' I felt a bit mean about it, I suppose, but sometimes you just feel great being alive, and I felt more alive because he wasn't alive anymore, because he would have gone to school with me, and now he couldn't, but I could. I've never had that feeling before, that it's great to be alive, but I had it then, and I've had it again . . . it gives things a bit more, I don't know . . . and when the lesson got really boring I thought that this is bad, but it's better than being dead.

Although there is no doubt that this boy felt very upset about the death of his friend, he also felt that that death had added flavour and significance to his own life. He also admitted that he had enjoyed the attention which he received through being the close friend of a victim of the disaster. It is worth remembering that bereavement has many aspects which are far from unpleasant.

How do schools react to disasters? As one might expect, the answer is in a variety of different ways. After the Hillsborough disaster a lot of schools started the week with the knowledge that some of their pupils were dead or seriously injured, and particular schools were hard hit with casualties. There seemed to be no general strategy for dealing with it. In some schools the head called the whole school together to discuss the event, but the emphasis in these cases was often on practical advice and the communication of details in connection with funerals, people in hospital and so on. Teachers were told to watch out for pupils who were seriously affected by the tragedy, but not given much idea about what if anything they were to do about it. It struck me at the time that it was not only the pupils who were in need of support; many of the teachers were obviously seriously affected by the disaster. There was a danger that their obligation to deal professionally with the problem as experienced by the pupils would lead them to ignore their own feelings.

Some schools did very little to discuss the disaster. The advice which teachers gave each other and pupils was to carry on as normal, or as far as one could carry on normally. Pupils were discouraged from talking about their experiences and feelings, and a strenuous effort was made to prevent the ordinary business of the school from being disrupted. The denominational schools did at least have rituals which helped them put the event in some sort of context, and staff were ready to deal with questions about how to reconcile religious faith with the death and suffering of so many innocent people. After all, this is a question which frequently arises anyway, and the only difference on this occasion is that its personal relevance became obvious. There is something which binds the members of the school together, namely, their religion, and although it is certainly true that the versions of a faith which may exist in such a school are quite diverse, there is a common factor which structures the activities of the school when very unusual situations arise. This factor does not have to be religion, but it can relate to a very strong local identity, or the ability of the school to forge a feeling of community out of a fairly disparate group of individual teachers and children. What is noticeable at times of disaster is that the schools which are capable of establishing a group identity are in a much stronger position to intervene and guide their members than similar schools which have not quite brought it off.

If this seems vague and woolly, then one must consider that the notion of a school being genuinely a 'community' school is far from clear, however popular that adjective might be. It is not difficult to tell quite quickly, though, whether a school really feels like a community, whether the individuals who are a part of it feel more than just isolated individuals who have been randomly gathered together with other similar individuals, or whether they feel like members of an institution which to some extent has their interests at heart. Some school managers are skilled at creating an atmosphere of community, while some schools just work as communities because of the attitudes of their members, and it is at times of crisis that the ethos of the school becomes important. A school which is not much of a community experiences a crisis as a threat to itself, since the links which hold its members together are quite tenuous and there is the feeling that anything out of the ordinary could shatter them. In such schools, the Hillsborough disaster was treated with embarrassment and dispatch. Managers were nervous at the implications which the disaster had for the smooth running of the institution and sought to ignore it as far as they could. By contrast, schools which are genuinely communities are strengthened by crisis. This is not to suggest that they welcome such events, quite the reverse, nor is it to suggest that they possess effective ways of dealing with them. What is true, though, is that the crisis can be incorporated into the normal running of the school because there is enough flexibility in the relationship between teachers, pupils and the local community to make this feasible. To give an analogy, a crisis in a relationship between two people can either strengthen that relationship or threaten it. A relationship which is strongly based is more likely to survive the crisis than one which is shaky. Precisely the same is true of complex institutions like schools, and a searching test of the nature of such institutions is provided when crises threaten.

Some schools, then, dealt with the disaster by trying to spend as little time as possible dealing with it. Some teachers were willing to talk about the disaster with the children – and all the children wanted to talk about it, especially those who had been involved – but others were not. These latter did respond to pupils' questions, but it was obvious that they were unhappy talking about the event, and they brought the conversation to an end as swiftly as possible. They did not encourage pupils to raise the topic again, and made frequent reference to the importance of getting back to work and not allowing the disaster to serve as an excuse for not working and behaving 'normally'. Even teachers who were fairly relaxed about discussing the event with pupils were decidedly more casual about their reactions when in the staffroom. Teachers on the whole wanted to give the impression of 'business as usual', and even the teachers who had personally been very much affected by the disaster did not let it show, or if they did let it show, they did all they could not to allow it to show too much. As one male teacher of around 40 told me:

I actually attended the match, so I saw some of the terrible things which happened, and I really did not feel like coming into school but everyone said I should get back to ordinary life as soon as possible so I came in. I did talk to the children about what I had seen, and how horrible it was, but I was reluctant to talk a lot about it . . . it had been so upsetting that I was frightened of breaking down and crying, especially when the children cried and stifled sobs. I really don't know how I got through that week. I didn't feel that I could talk about it with my colleagues. You spend so much of your time as a teacher coping, coping with difficult pupils, coping with the problems of constant change and reorganization, that you feel that you have to show that you can cope all the time . . . any sign of weakness, and you wonder if, well, people appear to be interested and sympathetic, but will the word get out that you are not really up to it?

This teacher reported that he went on to medication to help him carry on coping, something which again he felt he could not admit to his colleagues.

Not all teachers experienced this sort of attitude. A male teacher of the same age who had also been at the match reported:

When I went back to school the head had a word with me, and he sat me down and we had a long talk about Hillsborough. He told me that if I felt that I should like to stay off for a bit, this was fine, but that if I came in, he would really like me to talk to the children about what had happened. Everyone in the staffroom was really quiet, it was as if they were all mourning, and I don't know if you remember the atmosphere of the time, but it was as if the whole city was in mourning, and people were coming back from their classes with tears in their eyes. It was a terrible week, but by the end of it we all felt somehow closer together, as though we had gone through a major crisis and come out of it somehow stronger than we had started. No one could have gone through that week, and the weeks which followed, without being affected by it, without it changing them.

These interviews took place about nine months after Hillsborough, and they show the differences which exist in schools' attitudes to crises. It seems clear that there is a wide variety of approach in schools to such events, and this is as it should be, since different schools have different characters and they have to work out for themselves what sort of strategy is going to suit them. The teacher who found it hard to deal with his grief might have been in exactly the same situation had he been in a different sort of school, but it is perhaps not unlikely that the character of his school had a part to play in his subsequent difficulties. The attitude that the real feelings of teachers should be suppressed, that they should not allow those feelings to intrude in their work, is not very helpful when it comes to dealing with crises.

There are ways of advancing in the teaching profession, and when teachers talk to each other they pass on relevant information in this regard. They talk about how they dealt with difficult classes, how they organized their work and how they prepared material for an inspection, how they got on to a useful committee, and so on. Very little of this has anything directly to do with teaching, or with the nature of the relationship between teachers and pupils. Being able to hide one's feelings is a very important constituent of successful professional life, and teachers who allow themselves to be upset by what they find in the classroom, or indeed outside of it, are not going to be highly respected by their colleagues, and are unlikely to be seen as prime candidates for promotion. Teachers who exude the attitude, 'I am up to it!' and 'I don't crack under pressure' or 'Stressful circumstances do not get me down' are projecting the right sort of attitude for advancement. One can see the logic of this. There is little value in a school having teachers who are easily upset, who cannot cope with the everyday aggravations of teaching children who perhaps do not want to be there. Teaching is potentially a highly stressful occupation, and one has to be fairly tough to be a useful member of staff. If a teacher is open about his problems in coping with the work, it may have a detrimental effect upon his career. If the teacher requires counselling for those problems, then this may be offered by the employing authority but could easily be put on the teacher's record, and be an obstacle both to promotion and to moving to another job. Teachers are expected to get on with it, and if they find that they cannot cope with the work, then they should get out and do something less demanding.

All these issues come very much to a head when a crisis occurs. A crisis obliges us to examine whether our habitual reactions are appropriate to what turns out to be an abnormal situation. We can often no longer just react automatically to what has occurred, since the character of those events is so extraordinary as far as our experience goes. There comes a point at which the individual is unable to continue to counter stress successfully, and when that point is reached the individual will change. She may change her overt behaviour, or she may just change in other ways which come out later, but the result will be that she fails to function, in at least some aspect of her life, as effectively as she did before. A teacher may start to go sick a lot, snap all the time at the children and not concentrate upon her work. It is quite possible that her work will continue satisfactorily, but that her private life will be affected. It is far more efficient to seek to nip this sort of problem in the bud than to intervene when it reaches a serious stage.

It is not just the obligation that teachers are under to be seen to be coping which prevents them from being open about their feelings. It is also the fact that many teachers feel under a lot of pressure to get a lot done in relatively little time. Teachers spend a good deal of their professional life dashing around, and they seem to have very little time to discuss any problems they may have dealing with traumatic situations and their consequent stress, even at the level of casually talking with colleagues. A working life which is replete with constant business is not designed to allow the individual to reflect upon what is happening. It might even be suggested that much of this dashing about is specifically designed to prevent the teacher from having to consider the nature of what is taking place. It is often far easier to pretend to oneself that difficult issues which arise within one's relationships with pupils cannot be considered because there is just no time – the curriculum is too crowded and the teacher has far too many things to take on board for this additional consideration to have much weight. Teachers will say that they would love to do a whole variety of things with their pupils, but the problem of time gets in the way, and they have to stick to a more limited number of objectives. Now, it is obviously true that teachers do have a very busy schedule, and many teachers gain kudos from rushing breathlessly from one part of the school to the other. After all, this is evidence of how hard they are working, and, if they are in managerial roles, of how important they are to the running of the institution.

If one thing sticks in my mind from the many post-Hillsborough interviews of teachers which I held in the Merseyside region, it is the importance which so many of them ascribed to the atmosphere in the schools where they worked. What was particularly important was the attitude of other teachers, and of the school as a whole. If a teacher felt that he could sit down with his colleagues, or at least some of his colleagues, and discuss what they were feeling and how it was affecting them, then they came to think of the tragedy as something they could incorporate in their approach to the rest of their life. This is not to say that the tragedy is experienced as anything other than a tragedy, but it can be understood as having positive as well as negative consequences. For example, it may make people come closer together, and it may make them think of their lives in different ways which they come to see as having significant advantages over their former conceptions. Schools in which pupils and teachers felt that they could not be frank about their feelings, where they felt obliged to conceal their feelings, seemed rather unsuccessful in helping their members to deal positively with the tragedy. More pupils and teachers continued to blame Hillsborough for a whole sequence of psychological and physical problems even a long time after the event in such schools, and it is often a long time after the event that it becomes very important to be able to talk about it. Schools which were unsympathetic places for their members immediately after Hillsborough became far more so as time passed, yet many people came to need more support from the institution of the school than it was capable of giving.

For most people in our society, there is no obvious way to deal with a tragedy, since religious ritual is only accepted by a section of society, and one often wonders how far that section goes along with the world of the ritual. When one looks around at the faces of mourners at an Anglican funeral, for example, and listens to the clergyman saying 'in sure and certain knowledge of the resurrection', one often wonders whether the participants really have that belief. Rituals today have to be constructed out of more temporary materials than those provided by religion, and one of the most effective in the case of Hillsborough seems to be the coming together of people to discuss the event. There was a spontaneous outburst of grief in the city of Liverpool which manifested itself in the vast displays of scarves and flowers at Anfield, the home of Liverpool Football Club, and for quite a long time afterwards people got together and talked about the event. As we have seen, this also took place quite naturally in some schools, although in other schools there seem to have been determined moves to prevent it. Many pupils at the time and afterwards spoke about the support which they received from their peers, and sometimes from teachers, just by being able to talk about their experiences and the meaning of the event itself. The rituals which were created and which resulted in memorials of various kinds were also often felt to be valuable in helping survivors come to terms with their grief.

One school dealt with the matter of ritual in an interesting way. One of its pupils had been killed, and two injured, and the school asked the parents of the dead boy whether they could borrow some of his football regalia which they could put on show until they constructed a more permanent memorial. A 14-year-old boy, not a particular friend of the dead pupil, commented:

> I was dead surprised, because I thought the scarf and that would have been nicked, but they weren't, and we did think of him a lot when we passed it. Those weeks afterwards I remember, 'cos we spent lots of time talking about it, and who we knew who was hurt and that, and why it had happened . . . after a bit we didn't feel too bad about it.

In another school, which tried to make as little fuss as possible about Hillsborough, the pupils nonetheless spent a lot of time discussing it in the playground and out of school, and one 15-year-old girl made this perceptive comment:

> Because the teachers did not want to talk about it, it sort of made for a big gap between us, because we wanted them to talk to us about it, and they did not want to, and I think it was a shame since I am sure they cared, and in the end I thought that they weren't really interested in us, living in their posh houses and with their nice cars and that, they don't give a fuck really.

I think this comment is perceptive not because it provides an accurate description of the feelings of the teachers, but because it is a natural interpretation of the policy of not allowing teachers to get too close emotionally to the pupils when a crisis like Hillsborough arises. The divisions which already exist between staff and pupils are deepened even further, and that is hardly a positive step in the educational process.

An interesting aspect of crises is their publicity. This gives rise to the creation of rituals which help survivors and the bereaved cope with their grief. We have suggested that there are important implications for the way in which that grief will be experienced as a result of the approach of the school. A crisis presents death and injury in dramatic and public ways which of themselves are an aid to successful bereavement. During the discussions of Hillsborough a 13-year-old boy made this remark:

> I know it's terrible and all that, but I thought a lot about my mate Dan, whose mum has been dying of cancer for the last couple of years, and he had been living with that, visiting her in hospital, helping look after her at home, doing some of the shopping and that, and no-one apart from his friends and family know about it, only a few people are interested, and that must be really tough, 'cos he's entirely on his own, apart from a few of his friends, and he's got to live with it day after day . . . Hillsborough was terrible, yes, but the people who are involved in that they've got lots of others who are interested in them and who are talking about it all the time, but Dan's got nothing like that.

This brings us to a very important point. While a lot of publicity surrounds major tragedies, the most common tragedies are quite private and personal. Far more people experience private bereavements than are involved in the major public disasters. For them there is no extra attention or help. They are expected to get on with their lives as best they may regardless of the difficulties which they may be undergoing. If some teachers and pupils experienced little support after Hillsborough, one can imagine how likely they are to receive any support at all under less dramatic circumstances.

It is interesting to compare the experiences of people bereaved as a result of Hillsborough, and those bereaved through some more private event. The former on the whole seem to have emerged in a far more positive manner than the latter, and this is especially the case when one puts some distance between the time of the death and the eventual feelings of the people involved. The people bereaved through Hillsborough found that the cause of the deaths was much discussed, a commission of enquiry was set up, changes were made to the design of football stadiums as a consequence, and large public acts of mourning took place. Memorials were set up in several places, and the local press mentioned Hillsborough frequently even several years later, since it was not difficult to point to some vaguely relevant incident which was connected with the tragedy. A counselling service was set up soon after the disaster, and there are signs on the main motorway entrances to the city of Liverpool directing people to it. Compare this with the treatment of the ordinary individual who is bereaved as a result of a commonplace death. She is often largely isolated in her grief and lacking in any ritual which can meaningfully embody that grief. She may find it difficult to fit the death into a context which explains it, since it may seem to be arbitrary and without reason. What she needs is the support of a community prepared to talk with her about the dead person and about her feelings, but she is unlikely in contemporary society to live within such an environment. If she is at school, her problems are in some ways magnified. Her ability to understand what has taken place is under suspicion, and so is her awareness of what is involved in the bereavement process. It may be assumed that she is too young to be seriously affected by a death, and that her grief is necessarily limited by the optimism of youth, which will quite swiftly overcome her negative feelings. We have seen that these assumptions are highly questionable, so that the bereaved pupil has not only to cope with her grief, but also with the attitude that she will have few problems in doing so.

This is where schools can do a great deal to help the bereaved child. In contemporary society many people no longer know how to respond to bereavement except by way of embarrassment. They do not know what they are expected to say, or do, and they do not know how the bereaved person will react when they meet. The bereaved person does not know what forms of behaviour are appropriate on his part, and he does not know what he is supposed to do when he meets his friends, or how he should express his grief. When people live within a community, these problems do not arise to the same extent. This is because the individual feels that he knows how he should behave, and he feels that others are interested in his welfare and know about him. So there is far less artificiality in the relationships between people, and less scope for being worried that the other person will misinterpret one's words or actions. Schools can work as communities, and there may be an attitude in the school that all its members are part of an organic whole which is to some degree working together towards common goals. This atmosphere may have little to do with the teachers, but it can arise from the pupils, who may indeed come from a particular area and share in a variety of goals and ambitions. A community can be a very potent environment in which to assist bereaved people to come to terms with their grief. It need not be done in official and organized ways. Indeed, the most useful forms of support I have observed are the informal and spontaneous ways in which people who regard themselves as to some degree bound together make themselves available to discuss each other's problems and feelings.

While this sort of community may evolve quite naturally, those who organize schools cannot depend upon natural forces to create such an environment. As we have seen, many of the attitudes which are presently current in schools are profoundly unhelpful to both staff and students who are undergoing bereavement. Some schools seem to embody far more sympathetic approaches to members undergoing difficulties in adjusting to radically changed circumstances, and it would not be going too far to presume that these schools are going to be far more successful at doing the whole range of tasks which schools are today expected to accomplish. This is not to suggest that it is not possible to run a school which is successful academically but unsuccessful in other ways. This is obviously possible, and many teachers will have experience of such institutions. Academic success is not the only criterion of success of a school, though; even in the contemporary educational context schools are expected to do a lot more than just get children through examinations. In the discussion which is to come it will be argued that there are ways in which the topics of death and loss can be incorporated in the curriculum which have the potential to strengthen the ability of the school to deliver more reflective and responsible pupils into society at large. It is important to broaden the issue in this way, since otherwise it seems that we are calling for changes in the curriculum merely to respond to what surely is a rather small number of pupils and teachers who may be having difficulties in coming to terms with a particular form of stress: that arising from the death of someone close to them. But the issue is far broader than this. Far more is at stake than just the ability to deal successfully with the impact which death can have on our lives. What is at issue here is really how we should regard those lives themselves.

CHAPTER 7

Death in the curriculum

The evidence which has been produced so far suggests that schools do very little if anything to prepare children for the occurrence of death. This might not seem to be much of a problem. After all, there are many important topics which schools hardly cover at all, and it is often thought that controversial issues are best left out of the curriculum. They can perhaps best be dealt with at home by parents, and then they can be treated in the way that parents wish. There are so many interesting issues which schools could discuss, but do not because of shortage of time or expertise, and one might well wonder what reason there could be to push death to the head of the queue. A common objection would be that the curriculum is already so overcrowded with issues and problems which society wants teachers to raise that the introduction of yet another issue would compact still further the time available for a whole range of important matters. So many important issues never appear in the school timetable, so why give priority to death? Most teachers have a pet topic which they feel should play a larger part in the curriculum, and they can all produce good arguments for such additions. Is the topic of death just one more issue which teachers could discuss, along with a whole range of similar issues which impinge on the personal lives of pupils?

Then there is another point which has to be confronted, and this is how such a topic should be introduced into the curriculum. Should it be made part of the formal curriculum, or should it be treated as a special additional topic? This has serious implications for the way in which death might be studied. It could be made part of a whole range of subjects which are already taught in schools. On the other hand, it could be restricted to Personal and Social Education, which is itself a compulsory part of the formal curriculum. It is possible, also, for death to be dealt with by personal tutors in schools as and when the topic arises, as when children are bereaved, or by counsellors working with schoolchildren in specific circumstances. This is not just a technical issue, where the question is how to get over a particular set of ideas and concepts most efficiently. The way in which a topic is made part of the curriculum, or at least of what the educational system can provide, affects the ways in which it is received by pupils. It is not always possible to abstract the product of schooling from the process of delivery. For example, if a topic is treated as a part of the official teaching of a school it will make a different impression on pupils than if it is treated as an optional extra, and if that topic is made part of the examinable curriculum it will be regarded differently than if it is treated otherwise. One might expect that a topic which is fully integrated into the whole of the curriculum will have an impact which it could not have if it is treated as only part of that curriculum, or not part of the official curriculum at all. The analysis to which teachers submit a topic will tend to shape the way in which pupils experience the material they are expected to absorb. Something which teachers will often bear in mind is that the aims they have in introducing a particular subject will only be realizable if the means of dealing with it are appropriate to those aims.

Before we look at the variety of ways in which death might enter the curriculum, we should first discuss whether it should be introduced at all. Perhaps the reason why schools do very little if anything on this aspect of life is because it is not a topic which finds its right place in schools. Perhaps it is one of that large family of topics which could be made part of schooling, but which give rise to issues which are better dealt with elsewhere. A whole range of moral and political issues might be thought to come into this sort of category. It might be thought to be no part of the school's role to interfere with parents' control over such issues, since the values of parents should be respected and the school should not seek to impose its own values on the child. Parents might in any case wish schools to restrict themselves to the academic part of the curriculum, and not waste the time of their children in discussing superfluous topics. It certainly is noticeable that more 'academic' schools spend a far shorter time, if any time at all, on non-examination topics than do less academic schools. Brighter children are expected to have fewer problems with respect to sexual morality, drugs and crime, perhaps, than their less academic peers. The parents of the latter might be pleased to find that the school was prepared to tackle these issues with their children, if the parents are uneasy about dealing with such topics themselves. The parents of more academic children might have less interest in such issues, since their children are more likely to be at home working for their examinations and they are more likely to have absorbed middle-class values which will militate against certain kinds of risky behaviour. The interviews at the end of the book provide some evidence of this.

It could be argued that death is such an important topic that it should be brought into the school for discussion regardless of the academic abilities and interests of the pupils. Of course, the supporters of any topic not at present much discussed in schooling would find arguments to back up that topic's significance, but it would be difficult to find arguments which were stronger than those for the inclusion of death. Death is an event which will occur in everyone's life, and it is what might be called a key concept. A key concept is a concept which links together a network of other concepts in a crucial way. The other concepts which are involved here are, at the very least, those of risk and loss. Not only will we all die eventually, but we will all have to work out what our attitude to loss is and also what notion of risk we are going to adopt. Death is a symbol of what might be regarded as the ultimate loss, and it is the measure of the ultimate cost of risk. Talking about death enables us also to consider what our attitudes to loss and risk are, and how we should develop our thinking in relevant ways.

Now, it might seem that this is far too dramatic a way of characterizing what might be quite minor events. For example, it seems hardly appropriate to compare not getting the qualifications I want with death, or losing my favourite bicycle with death. Similarly, if I am considering whether I ought to leap on to a moving bus, or try to pass an examination without doing much work, then these risky activities seem to have no connection with death. In a sense this is true, and it would be ridiculous to expect the individual to consider what links exist between what they are considering and their death in such cases. Yet there is a connection. Contemplating death involves thinking about what it would be to lose everything, to continue no longer, to have something happen to one which brings everything to an end. As such it is pedagogically very relevant, in that it presents in graphic fashion what is involved at the limit of human action and being. If we are able to consider our own death with equanimity, then we are in a better position to consider calmly losing less serious possessions than our lives. This does not imply that an appropriate attitude to such relatively minor loss need be a calm one. There are circumstances in which it is surely highly appropriate for us to become very angry and upset, but it does enable us to put such reactions within a broader context if we have been able to confront the notion of loss in the past. Thinking about death, and indeed about our own death, helps us to think about our attitude towards loss in general.

Is this really the case? What reason is there to think that just because someone is able to contemplate his own death, he is then better able to contemplate suffering a loss, or indeed actually suffer the loss? There is no reason to think that this has to happen, but a good deal of what goes on in school is founded on the idea that making something more vivid to pupils will help them to relate it to their own lives. If one is able to get pupils to empathize with the characters in a play, for example, or with historical figures, they will find it easier to imagine what it would be like for them to be in a similar situation. One of the problems about thinking about death in our society is that it is such a familiar feature of the media in the form of fake deaths on television or in print that it is difficult to think about it clearly as something which can happen to oneself. A way of trying to understand it is by trying to understand what happens when something is lost, when one of a person's projects is sidetracked or goes awry. Major losses are often described in very similar terms to death, and sometimes lead quite directly to death in that the loss is regarded as so major that there is no prospect of acceptable life afterwards. We can use the concept of loss to help us understand the concept of death, and vice versa. Since death is a notion whose other side we cannot observe, as it were, given that we do not live to tell the tale, we require the concept of loss to help us work out what it means to us.

This might seem to be a circular argument, since previously it was suggested that the concept of death is involved in the concept of loss. But what we have here are notions which are irretrievably connected, so that it is often difficult to distinguish between them. Death is the epitome of loss, the perfect example of what it is to lose something, and as such it plays a vital role in the definition of loss. But is loss such an important topic that it is incumbent upon schools to deal with it? It shares with death the characteristic of universality. Everyone will lose things, everyone will have ambitions which will be unrealized, everyone will encounter setbacks in life. It has often been argued that our society is death-denying, and although this opinion has been criticized, it has also been argued that there is some truth in the claim. Our society is certainly not as open in its discussions of death as have been some earlier societies. Our society is certainly a loss-denying society. Consumerism has as its main symbol of value the acquisition of possessions, and success is measured in terms of the things which one can have and own. We identify ourselves with our possessions and with our occupations, and we find it difficult to feel any sense of who we are without those roles and things. Anything which schools can do to help pupils think critically about the values of such a society is useful, and one of the most potent illustrations which teachers can use is that of death, the ultimate loss of possessions, of everything.

Children are heavily affected by the ethos of consumerist society. They are after all acquiring the social norms which are widely shared by adults and are trying out a variety of forms of behaviour until they find one which satisfies them. Young people who steal will quite frequently explain their actions in line with the idea that they deserve to have things even if they cannot afford to have them. This conversation with a 15-year-old boy in Tyneside who, like his friends, often steals cars is by no means untypical:

> I can get into a car really quickly, and then I drive it around for a bit with my mates . . . and what I really like is other drivers looking at me and thinking that it's my car, that I'm like them. Why shouldn't I have a car? I mean, you see cars on the TV all the time, lots of people have them, why shouldn't I have one? When I see something I want, if I can take it, I'll have it. Why shouldn't I? There's no work round here, I won't get a job, I'll never have the cash to buy things like that. You have to have things, because if you don't have things you're not a person, you're nothing, you're rubbish. I suppose when I've got things like that, stolen I mean, I'm sort of pretending that I'm like the people who really own them, but I'm cleverer than they are, 'cos I can just take things off them. Everyone does it round here.

What is interesting about this statement, and many similar reports, is that the young person does not appear to feel any guilt about his actions.

He feels that as a member of this society, he is entitled to the possessions which people in our society usually own, the things he feels are rightfully his. He is not prepared to put up with the loss of these things just because of his poverty. It might be thought that 'loss' is not the right description here, since the thief never really owned that which he took. But loss is a very appropriate description, in the sense that the young person feels that he deserves to have a certain amount of wealth and if he does not have it, then he experiences its absence as a loss. He has lost what goes with being a member of our society, the things which any citizen is persuaded he has a right to own.

Teachers who confront pupils like this are in a very difficult position. They can tell the pupils that it is wrong to do what they are doing, but this is hardly likely to be very effective. The pupil does seem to believe quite genuinely that she is entitled to whatever it is that she steals, since as a member of our society she cannot really be herself without it. Such pupils experience absence of crucial possessions as a loss, and if they are bold enough they may seek to replace that loss at someone else's expense. Now, it might be argued that what we have here is just a number of children who are inclined to steal, which is hardly anything novel. There have always been dishonest, violent and avaricious young people, and it is the task of teachers to warn them of the consequences of such illegal and undesirable behaviour. What is required in such cases is not to work with pupils on a mutual understanding of the concept of loss, but to persuade them of the error of their ways. This should be done both from a moral perspective, so that the teacher reinforces the moral norms of our society in the pupils, and also pragmatically, since the negative consequences of the social sanctions against crime should be emphasized. This was certainly the way in which such topics would have been dealt with in the past, and it seems just common sense to treat them similarly today.

There have, however, been important changes both in schools and in society in the last two decades. Given the fact of high youth unemployment, schools no longer qualify their pupils for work as they did in the past and the norms of the teacher-pupil relationship which existed in the past no longer obtain. Whereas in the past pupils subjected themselves to authority in order to acquire information which would increase their value on the labour market, today the position is different. Young people know that even if they do relatively well at school they may have difficulties in getting paid employment and all that goes with it. In addition, the previous social attitude that life is hard to bear has been progressively dissipated. As Marcuse puts it, the values of the sphere of production have lost significance in Western society. These values were linked to delaying satisfaction and restraining desire, and now they are to be replaced with values connected with the sphere of consumption and the pleasure principle, i.e. instant gratification of desires, lust, happiness, and the absence of repression (Marcuse, 1966). It would be wrong to regard the transformation from one value system to another as having been a smooth and universal process. It is still possible to find schools with middle-class values which hark back to previous times, where there is an emphasis on strictly controlled behaviour, mastery of emotions and impulses, feelings of guilt and fear of authority. Children who go to such schools will be powerful competitors in modern society, and they are likely to perform well on the traditional academic curriculum. Such schools are not the norm any longer, though, since most schools will contain predominantly working-class pupils who are submerged in the ethics of consumption, and who regard the values of self-discipline, obedience, order, subservience, diligence, punctuality and stamina as alien to them.

Another important feature of contemporary society is that it is rapidly changing, so that adults have very different lives from their parents, and children can expect that their lives as adults will be very different from the lives of their parents. This means that the transfer of culture through tradition will not be as relevant in the future as it was in the past. Thus we see the creation of what some have called the postmodern society, which is ambiguous, unclear and often shapeless. It is supposed to contrast with modern society, which is organized on rational lines, where the whole population is at work and where the goal is growth and material improvement. Modern society thinks it knows where it is going, it has a direction, but postmodern society is by contrast directionless, and adheres to no transcendent values or beliefs. This has important implications for the notion of identity, for whereas in the past young people inherited their future from their parents, today this is far less possible. This gives young people a lot more freedom to choose their own futures, but far less of a context of solid ritual and strategies of survival within which to make such choices. Since postmodern society has as its conception of the goal of life an endless pursuit of new experiences, values and vocabularies, and no conception of human nature or the fixed self, it is going to provide no framework within which decisions can be constructed. It is up to the individual to do what she wants. This may be experienced as very liberating. On the other hand, it may appear to be chaotic, and lead the individual to follow his impulses and to seek the continuous pursuit of external stimuli. The difficulties of structuring one's own lifestyle and building one's identity may be resolved by accepting what the leisure industry has to offer in terms of immediate, intense and exciting images. If there are no objective criteria of value, then style becomes crucially significant, since style is created by us and can embody our hopes and ambitions. Style is significant because it increases the intensity of our feelings, and those feelings enhance our sense of being alive. What is important is what is happening now.

Schools in postmodern society are different places from what they were in the quite recent past. They have lost their traditional cultural support and legitimation, and if they are to work they have to forge new contexts of meaning and relationships with their members. It may seem that the changes which postmodernity has brought in its wake are all going to be highly destructive of the sorts of things which schools need to do, but this is not necessarily the case. Schools have to channel values like enjoyment, excitement and change into creativity, spontaneity and the realization of the self. It is no longer possible for schools to treat knowledge as an economic resource or as a value to be encashed for goods such as increased production, competitiveness, improved examination passes, promotion, higher pay and so on. There needs now to be a concern for personal development, for the ways in which the individual shapes her life in everyday contexts and constructs her personality. How is the young person to carry this out in positive ways? It seems quite difficult, since there are no firm rules which define what is permissible, and there is a deficiency of experience on which they can draw. There is certainly a danger that postmodern society will develop an inevitable dependence on the stimuli of its environment, especially those coming from the media. Teachers should help young people stay clear of such dependence and give them room to work out who they want to be. It would go against the principles of postmodernity, though, for teachers to imply that they know what young people should become, since it is very much up to the individual to construct his own identity. When governments and parents hark back to a lost golden age (the slogan 'Back to Basics' comes to mind here) they are just refusing to acknowledge the radical changes which society has undergone. It is not possible to recreate the past in the present if the present is very distinct from the past.

One of the features of postmodern society which puzzles many teachers is precisely its postmodernity. They may have been brought up within a very different structure, and they are then confronted with pupils who do not appear to share their attitudes. This is a perfect recipe for lack of communication. Teachers may refer their pupils to old certainties which no longer apply to their pupils. What the latter require is some practice in working out for themselves what sort of people they are going to become, and teachers have an important role here in creating room for young people to discuss and analyse a variety of ideas and alternatives. There is no reason to think that teachers do not have anything to contribute to such a process. For one thing, teachers are interested in showing their pupils how to think for themselves, at least in the sense of not allowing them to be dominated by the media and its values. The difference from the past form of teaching is that in a postmodern society young people must be more active with what they learn. They cannot just use it to exchange for something else, like a job or praise from parents, but have to make it part of their developing conception of who they are. This calls for a different pedagogy, one which emphasizes active learning and the autonomy of the learner. Naturally, many teachers who were themselves brought up as part of a very different process may find such methods unfamiliar and threatening, yet it is only through such methods that postmodern children can be taught.

This might seem to be a wild over-exaggeration. Surely there are many schools which successfully follow principles and methods of teaching which strongly resemble those of the past. There are also many teachers who teach in much the same way as they were taught, and to the great benefit of their pupils. This is all true. It is an error to treat society as entirely homogeneous, with social changes affecting every aspect of that society in similar ways. We have already seen that class certainly affects the rate at which such changes influence different sections of society, and no doubt there are many other factors which are also significant. The debate over postmodernism has succeeded in highlighting certain features of contemporary society which have come to have growing influence. There is little doubt that many of the changes which have been described here can be observed to some extent in British schools, and they have led to schooling becoming a far more strenuous process for both teachers and pupils. The expectations and experiences which in the past could be taken for granted are no longer there to the same extent, and the relationship which existed between teachers and pupils has to be reconstructed if it is to be effective. Although such a suggestion might be regarded as problematic, since we can no longer rely on the traditional ways of doing things which once obtained, it could also be used to create new opportunities for education in a positive sense. Teachers and pupils are required to think clearly about how they are going to work together, and this can only be to the mutual advantage of everyone in the educational process.

Talking about death, loss and risk with pupils is an excellent example of what is possible in postmodern schools. When we looked at some of the problems involved in discussing risk with pupils, the point was made that there is no objective standard of risk when it comes to deciding how much risk is acceptable to a particular individual. Some people are happy to work within a high level of risk, while others are far more risk-averse. In many ways it is a matter of taste. Teachers saw the activities of many of their pupils as being often highly risky, while the pupils put this down to the boring and cautious lifestyle of their teachers. Now, there is certainly scope for discussing the levels of risk which apply to different activities, and this sort of discussion can be quite objective, but it is up to the individual to decide how much risk is acceptable to her. She may come to change her mind and wonder at her recklessness when young, but it is her decision to adopt a certain attitude to risk. It is part of what makes her the sort of person she is. Teachers can contribute some understanding of the facts to this sort of discussion and also some experience of how commercial forces in society may succeed in persuading young people to discount risk in favour of a certain lifestyle. For example, teachers are more aware of the facts behind the dangers of cigarette smoking than are most teenagers, and they are also aware of the ways in which the tobacco industry has managed to persuade a lot of young people that it is smart to smoke. They can then in discussing smoking with teenagers present this sort of information for their consideration. But if after having given these facts some thought, the teenagers wish to continue, or start, smoking, there is not much that the teacher can do. Young people, especially those of 16 and over, have the right to participate in any legal activity, and it is not acceptable for older and 'wiser' people to intervene and oblige them to behave in ways which may be more conducive to their wellbeing. This sort of behaviour has as its appropriate context the sort of schooling which existed in the past, when the teacher as an authority figure could rely upon a degree of obedience and subservience in his pupils. It does not apply today, and any attempt to mould the pupil to the ideas of the teacher would be an exercise in replicating the ways in which the media seek to mould the child to follow its demands. Both attempts interfere with the autonomy of the individual and prevent the individual from working out in his own way how he is going to react to the pressures which society applies.

Exactly the same sort of thing can be said about loss. There is no right or wrong way to treat loss, there is just the way which fits in with the beliefs and attitudes of the individual. Some people will treat a relatively minor loss in a highly dramatic fashion, whereas others will remain calm and collected. Some young people will accept that there are things which they cannot afford and so cannot have, and they will not regard the absence of such possessions as a loss, while others will be angry at what they come to regard as the loss of that to which they feel entitled, and they may take steps to help themselves to other people's property in order to rectify what they regard as an imbalance. While one could certainly produce an argument against stealing, it is not similarly possible to argue against regarding absence of certain things as a loss. One might say that if one has not earned the money or been given those things, then it is wrong to regard their absence as a loss, but such arguments will not be appreciated by those whose self-concept is strongly connected with such things, and who regard their culture as insisting that they have them. As we have seen, it is very much an axiom of postmodern society that the most important system of ethics is the ethic of consumption: if we are unable to consume, then we are not really people. The inability to consume is treated just as much like a loss as would the lack of a job in a previous time, given that members of this society feel that they are entitled to consume as a result of their membership of society. One cannot argue objectively from a position of ownership against such a view, since it is very much the sort of view which is part and parcel of living in our society. As such there are no objective criteria of ownership, just ways in which people regard that to which they are entitled.

Yet we can confront this notion of loss and subject it to a critique in the classroom. We can discuss the ways in which we are persuaded that we ought to have certain things, and we can argue that young people should think about the pressures which influence them in this respect. This would be a very similar sort of argument to that when we address the notion of risk, when perhaps we are looking at the ways in which the tobacco industry helps persuade young people to buy their products. We cannot oblige young people to reject the influences which urge them to consume, since that would be to go against the whole direction in which our society is moving, and in any case we would not want to impinge on their freedom of choice. On the other hand, as teachers we should like to enable them to view as objectively as possible the ways in which society tries to get them to do things and want things, since we want them to have the space in which to step back from that situation and see if it accords with their wishes. It might seem that what is being advocated here is a quietist position, the sort of attitude in political theory according to which one just puts up with what happens. This would be to try to persuade young people that if they do not have the sorts of things which other people have, then they should reconcile themselves to their relative lack of possessions and not seek to acquire them, or at least not by illegal means. They should accept their poverty and not concern themselves over the relative inequalities in society, because that is just how things are. Not only would such an approach not work, but it is very far from what is being suggested here. It is no part of the role of the teacher to persuade young people to accept their lot. It is, on the other hand, part of that role to persuade them to consider critically what things they think they ought to have, and how important those things are to their sense of identity.

It might appear that what is being suggested here is far too difficult for schools to accomplish. Teenagers have a great desire to conform to their image of the norm, and it is surely a Herculean task to try to get them to view that norm from an external point of view. It is not difficult for teachers to do this, since they are distanced from that norm through their age and position in the school, and they may have values very different from those of their pupils. On the other hand, young people are often happy to discuss the pressures on them to conform in various ways, and they are capable of observing those pressures quite objectively. A 10-year-old boy in Manchester was commenting with some degree of sophistication on the fact that the football team he supports changes its official strip every year.

> Well, what they do is, they change the official strip every year, and sometimes more than once a year, to get all the lads to have to buy new strips, and I would hate to be seen out in the old strip, even if it has just gone out. It marks you out, you can't afford to keep up with the changes if you have to stick with the old strip. It's a rip-off really, but what can you do? You have to do it, and my parents moan about it, of course, and I can see their point. . . . When you think about it, it's wrong, and I get angry about it sometimes. I don't think I'll always want to go along with the changes, I think in the end I'll keep on supporting the team but wear a neutral strip. I don't like being taken for a mug.

It is a mistake to think that children are uncritical about the ways in which the commercial world seeks to manipulate them. In particular, they can analyse and deconstruct advertisements on television with a remarkable degree of skill and self-awareness. They are, after all, the intended audience, and they can take an objective view of what measures are taken by advertisers to try to get them to buy the products. This is an area of debate which teachers can very productively exploit. They can thereby improve children's natural capacity to take control of what is happening to them.

Teachers should not, then, try to persuade young people that they can put up without the normal amount of possessions of people in their society. Such attempts would be futile. Teachers would be seeking to counteract the influences of consumer society, and they are heavily outgunned in such a contest. Young people will already in most cases have a firm idea of what they think they ought to have, and it is pointless to attack that concept directly. If young people experience the absence of certain things as a loss, then there is little that teachers can do to alter their opinion. What they can do is encourage a discussion of loss which is capable of bringing up issues that might lead to a consideration of how we should deal with loss. Now, one of the points we have made about loss is that it is very similar to risk in that there is no objective criterion of what a reasonable attitude to either notion is. It is up to the individual to work out for himself what attitude he is going to adopt, and the best thing that the teacher can do is provide him with the conceptual and factual materials to construct as rational an attitude as possible. This will not be done by hectoring the young person to share the teacher's attitude, but it could be done by giving him the impression that the teacher is genuinely interested in finding out how he is going to arrive at a particular point of view.

One of the features of contemporary schooling that I have noticed when sitting in classrooms is that discussions of issues like this are often very poorly conducted. When the teacher asks for pupils' views, two things often happen. One is that the teacher just elicits a number of views and does not subject those views to analysis. In addition, the teacher is seen to listen to the views of the pupils, but with a closed mind. There is no way that the teacher is going to change his views despite the observations of his pupils. Neither reaction is helpful. These sorts of reactions do at least have the virtue that the teacher does not intervene in the discussions to lay down the law, as it were, but his failure to respect the arguments of the pupils puts him at a disadvantage. In the first sort of case, where the teacher encourages the pupils to give their opinions but does nothing with them, there is no real attempt at finding out what the pupils think. It has the appearance of being such an enterprise, but the reality is different. When we want to know what someone thinks we do not just ask them to produce an opinion. We want to know how they reconcile that opinion with their other views, and we challenge the view if we disagree with it. This is what is involved in respecting the views of others. We treat the information which we receive about the opinion as leading us to consider the opinion's validity. We do not just treat it as information about what is going through someone's head. That sort of psychological information is interesting, but its interest has little to do with the quality of the opinions, only with who has them. When teachers encourage children to produce their opinions, and end up by hearing from everyone in the class, they have not really elicited the views of the class. All that they have done is to get the pupils to produce some statement which is then replaced by another statement from the next pupil. This is very different from listening to the views of the class and treating them as interesting and worth considering. Pupils quickly pick up this lack of interest, and they come to treat presenting their views with an appropriate degree of cynicism.

But might it not be that the views of the pupils are not really interesting, and so the teacher is treating them quite rightly with a degree of casualness? Yet what is worth noting here is that the views of the pupils *are* interesting, because they are an attempt at explaining their ideas about themselves. This is true of the family of concepts connected with death, loss and risk. When the pupil talks about his attitude to these concepts, he is talking about important aspects of the sort of person he wants to become. For example, if a pupil says that he is unconcerned about the risks of smoking or unsafe sex, that he regards a particular failure as closing off a whole range of options, and that he has not thought at all about the nature of his own death, this presents the teacher with an excellent summary of what the pupil thinks about a range of crucial topics. That range plays a large part in defining the views of the pupil on the person he thinks he is and how he expects to behave. The pupil is reporting on how he sees the world, what the characteristics of his world are. Even if what he has to say is not especially original or exciting, it is still interesting to find out how he is thinking and what sort of decisions he is making. It is interesting not only because it gives us an insight into the way he is thinking, but it is also relevant to the teacher's own way of thinking. That is, the teacher has to work out himself what his attitude is going to be to this range of issues, and unless he is prepared to listen seriously to a variety of approaches, he is going to be guilty of adopting an attitude uncritically.

This is why it is important for the teacher to be open to the opinions of his pupils. There are certainly many aspects of the curriculum where a teacher plays a sort of game with the pupils in which he pretends that he does not know the answer, and the pupils pretend that they think that the teacher does not know the answer. This sort of approach can be useful, in that it can help pupils work out the answer for themselves with occasional guidance from the teacher. Sometimes this is called discovery learning, but it is not really discovery learning at all, in the sense that what is being discovered is already well known, although not to the pupils. What is interesting in such a teaching process is developing in young people the capacity to work through to the answer by themselves, or as independently as possible. When it comes to discussing topics like death and loss, by contrast, what is interesting is not only how the pupils work out their conclusions, but also the conclusions themselves. Teachers know no more than their pupils what the conclusions should be. Teachers can certainly recognize howlers in reasoning more readily than pupils, on the whole, and they probably have a better grasp of the facts, but this is not enough to rank their conclusions higher than their pupils'. Teachers, like pupils, have to develop what they regard as an appropriate attitude to such issues, and both parties should be interested in what the other has to say.

It may seem that the conclusions which one might reach in this area are not assessable rationally, since apparently anything goes. That is, if a young person says that smoking now has a greater value to him than a longer and healthier life, then he is presenting his values and

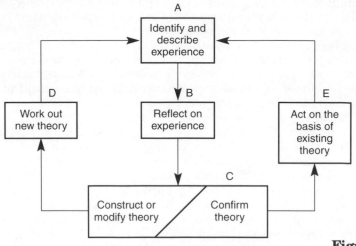

Figure 7.1

vision of his life in a way which may surprise his teacher, but the latter can do nothing to show that such a position is irrational or necessarily unsatisfactory. If rationality does not enter into the discussion, then surely it does not matter what pupils or teachers say in defence of their views, since they are just presenting what are personal views, akin to discussing what they prefer to eat for breakfast in the morning. This would be going too far, however. Reason does enter the picture in the sense that it is incumbent upon the individual to work out rationally how the various parts of the picture hang together. They have to take steps to show that they understand the implications of what they are arguing, so that there are no inconsistencies in the description of a life which they are presenting. This can best be explained by giving examples of actual conversations which try to do this.

I have already given examples in the book of the sort of things pupils say in defence of their behaviour, and there are some detailed accounts in the appendix of particular conversations with groups of pupils. What we require is some theoretical framework which would allow us to understand better what is happening in such contacts between pupils and teachers, and how teachers could intervene more effectively in such conversations. It is helpful to construct a model of the stages in an experiential learning cycle to help us grasp the different aspects of what is taking place and what might occur (see Figure 7.1). The model has been put together in this way because the object is to investigate how pupils learn from experience, and how that learning could be improved. The first stage is that of identifying and describing a particular experience. This is the total response of the individual to a situation or event, and represents what she thinks, feels, does and concludes at the time and just afterwards. Paradoxically, it is often difficult to identify what the experience really is while actually immersed in it, and if the cognitive process ends with or soon after the experience, the knowledge attained may remain tacit and be difficult to access. Reflection thus becomes very important. The individual needs to deal critically with a previous activity or experience, to think about thinking. This does not imply that she has to stop participating in that activity, or in any other activities, in order to think about it. It is often possible to reflect upon an experience while still having it, but it is important that the individual has the capacity to distance herself from what is going on to a certain extent so that it can be assessed and considered outside of its immediate context.

What is referred to here as a theory is really quite simple, since it represents the ways in which people try to anticipate through reflection what actions will lead to what consequences. It is personal to an individual and is continually tested throughout life. As the consequences are observed it is necessary to decide which theories need to be altered and modified, and which come out as successful for the individual. Some individuals who observe that the consequences are not as they expect will go to stage D, while others who are satisfied will go to stage E on the diagram. It is important that they then go on to stage A, to use the theory to make sense of the experience, since only then will they make the theory part of their everyday thinking. They will have learnt from their experiences, and they will relate that learning to the experiences themselves. What we have here is a process which operates constantly, and it is difficult to separate the various stages from each other, since we operate on such a model without clearly differentiating between the stages or noticing that this is the way we think. Outlining such a model could be useful in helping decide how teachers are going to try to intervene in the lives of their pupils, at least in so far as the network of concepts connected to death is concerned.

Let us take as an example the experience of unprotected sex. Pupils may describe this experience quite graphically, and say what it is about it which they find enjoyable. It is important that the teacher encourages the pupils to move onto stage B, since otherwise they will remain stuck with the experience alone. What often happens, of course, is that teachers are so indignant about what pupils tell them that they prevent a move on to stage B by directly challenging the acceptability of stage A. It is preferable to encourage pupils to reflect on the experience, which leads inevitably to the stage where they consider the theory which makes sense of what happened. This is where pupils are encouraged to think of the consequences of what took place, what led to it and what it in turn might lead to. Now they have two routes in front of them. They can either decide that they should modify their behaviour, and so not return to doing the same thing in the same way again, or they may decide that there are no problems with repeating their behaviour. In the latter case the same behaviour will recur. What is important about this process from an educational point of view is that pupils learn to put what they do within a wider context, that they reflect upon their practice. This is all that teachers can expect of pupils, and it is not easy to accomplish.

Some of the teachers with whom I was working tried out this sort of model, and the results are interesting. This conversation with a 15-year-old boy in the Midlands, called Joe, went in this way:

> *Joe*: Well, it was not my first time I went with a girl, but I did not use anything. . . .
>
> *Teacher*: (The teacher did not do anything or make any remark at all, but indicated that he was interested in hearing what Joe had to say about what happened.)
>
> *Joe*: It all happened so fast, like, and I was worried that if I started to talk about condoms and that, she would have cleared off. . . . I suppose if I'd had one with me, I might have used it, but I didn't have one and she didn't seem to expect me to.
>
> *Teacher*: When you say that you might have used protection what do you mean? Do you think that what you did was dangerous?
>
> *Joe*: Yeah, well what I did was a bit chancy. She could have got pregnant or I could have got AIDS.
>
> *Teacher*: And perhaps both things could have happened?
>
> *Joe*: Yes, they could've, but they didn't and you've got to take some risks, don't you? I mean, if you worry about everything, you'd never do anything, and if you say to a girl I've got to use a condom she might think, 'Oh, I wonder what's up with him' and it'd put her off.
>
> *Teacher*: It could be that she would be impressed that she would be looked after by you, though.
>
> *Joe*: Yeah, well, she wasn't that type of girl. I mean, I don't think she was that bothered.
>
> *Teacher*: Perhaps then you were at risk because she might have not bothered who she had been with before you, and you might have been infected by her?
>
> *Joe*: Well, I wasn't worried, and she wasn't worried.
>
> *Teacher*: Do you now think that you ought to be worried?
>
> *Joe*: No, not really. If you worried about everything you'd never do nothing, would you?

This is a good example of a pupil being encouraged to reflect upon his experience, as a result of which he did not feel that his original theory required altering. Some might regard the conversation as a failure because of this conclusion, but this would be wrong. What Joe has done is to put his actions within a wider context and examine them. He has been led to express his views on risk and on how that affects his behaviour towards other people. He has been provided with some facts which he may have either not known previously or which he may have discounted. It was my impression at the interview, and the impression of his teacher, that he was responding honestly to what he was asked. He was not presenting us with the answers which he felt we wanted to hear. I am not suggesting that Joe's responses are morally satisfactory, nor that the matter should be left there. There is plenty of scope for bringing the topic up again with him, and for inviting him to develop some of the points which he made. But from the point of view of getting Joe to articulate his views, and especially his views on risk, the interview was a success. Joe had to reflect on his actions, and what the result of that reflection will eventually turn out to be may be very different from what it was here.

This is the whole point of talking about death and risk in school. It obliges pupils to consider their position on these issues, and how that position links up with their behaviour. It does not oblige them to alter their behaviour or their views, but this is not the role of the teacher. That role is to invite pupils to consider rationally what it is that they are doing and why. Once pupils can understand what the bases of their actions are, or at least express what they think they are, they are in a position to understand those actions, and to take more informed decisions about them. From a moral point of view it is unclear how far a teacher should try to force a pupil to change his behaviour. In the case of Joe, who has been committing what is an illegal act, the teacher should of course point this out and also produce any moral arguments which he might have to show what is wrong with that act, but it is questionable whether this would be effective. What the teacher wants to do is get the pupil to work out himself what is wrong with his behaviour, not just because of its possible consequences for himself, but also because of what it can do to others. A direct assault on the moral conscience of the pupil is unlikely to be successful. A more indirect approach which helps the pupil work out the real character of his behaviour for himself is often more profitable.

Often teachers adopt the façade of being an expert, of knowing everything and always being correct. This can be very unproductive in their contact with pupils. There certainly are many areas about which teachers have a better understanding than do their pupils. But there are areas of experience and behaviour where teachers are not experts, and should not pretend to be experts. Teachers who spent their youth in a pre-AIDS environment have to be very careful in identifying their own youthful sexual experiences with those of their pupils. Teachers who grew up in a modern culture have to be wary about regarding their experiences as similar to those of someone growing up in a postmodern society. This is not a counsel of despair, or a claim that teachers cannot understand the lives of their pupils and so should not get involved in discussing their pupils' actions. On the contrary, it is vital that teachers find out and discuss how the world seems to be for their pupils. What it does mean, though, is that teachers have to be very aware that their pupils' experience of the world can be very alien to their own experience, and so they have to find out what is going on. When it comes to attitudes to death, to risk and to loss there are no experts, only a variety of views. It is up to teachers to encourage pupils to reflect on their experiences, and this has to be done in a subtle and non-judgmental way.

It is not only in these sorts of cases that pupils should be encouraged to learn by reflecting on their practice, of course. There are many cases in which such learning is desirable, and teachers will often try to stimulate such enquiry. If children can reflect on their own experience, their learning can be made much more real to them. It will be seen to connect with their lives, and not be abstract and irrelevant information which one has to pretend to acquire at school and which can be discarded when no longer required. Many pupils can be encouraged to develop a capacity for reflection, and the reflective process can be represented as a means of active learning. They are often willing to confront and dwell on their own fallibilities and imperfections. In this way they make an honest attempt to deal with them, to develop their own insights and come to value their mistakes as well as their achievements. Let us take as another example this conversation in the same school in the Midlands that Joe attended, but this time with a girl we shall call Sue:

Sue: Well, I went to this party, and I got a bit drunk, and after a bit I sort of ended up on this bed having sex with this boy I know a bit, and afterwards I felt really bad about it, because we had not used anything, and anything could have happened.
Teacher: What do you think you wanted to happen when you went to the party?
Sue: I wanted to have a laugh, see my mates and have a few drinks, but nothing like that; I mean, I know it's dodgy to go with someone you don't know and I don't do that usually, I don't know why I did then.
Teacher: Perhaps it had something to do with the amount you drank, and losing control as a result?
Sue: Yeah, well that's what happened. It's funny, though, 'cos I really like to stay in control over what I do, and it sort of shows that you can't stay in control and get drunk.
Teacher: Does that mean that in future you won't get drunk?
Sue: No, I think that's going a bit far. I won't get drunk when there are lads around, because you don't know what will happen then.... I think it's OK if it's just girls having a laugh.
Teacher: What is it about drinking that you enjoy?
Sue: I like it when you feel all blurry and happy, and you don't really know what's going on. You sort of forget who you are. But you've got to be careful where you do it. I don't want to get into that sort of situation again.

As a result of reflecting on her experience, Sue had developed a new theory which she was going to use to change her behaviour. She realized that what she enjoyed about drinking was not connected with some of the actions which drink tended to generate, and she was going to try to drink within a context that excluded those actions. Or so she said. One cannot tell whether she was sincere in her claims. It may be that she was not unwilling to participate in sex while drunk, and that she enjoys that sort of context within which to behave. What is important is that she is given the opportunity to reflect upon her experience, so that it is not something she accepts uncritically. She understands that it is up to her how she behaves, and that if she engages in certain kinds of behaviour, a number of consequences are likely to follow. This need not alter her behaviour, but it gives her a theory about that behaviour which she cannot ignore when she comes to act again. Of course, she may deceive herself about the consequences of her actions, or she may through weakness of will not act as she originally wished, and when she reflects upon her experience these are issues which could arise for her. If, for example, she sets out to reach a certain goal and never manages to accomplish it, she may wonder whether something quite basic is going wrong with her theory of action, which might then require modification. She has to think about what she does, and as a result of that thinking she is in a position to understand better why she behaves the way she does.

This does not mean that it is the role of teachers to nag their pupils about their imprudent behaviour, although many teachers do seem to operate in that way. Authoritarian teaching behaviour is unlikely to be effective anyway. The pupil will tend to switch off when the teacher talks to him, and there will be a lack of frankness in their communication. The result may well be that the pupil fails to reflect on his experience, or only does it to a limited degree, and the teacher then becomes dismissive about the potential of the pupil to take sensible decisions about his life. The teacher can then wash her hands of the pupil, as it were, in that she can say that she has done all that she can do, and if the pupil wishes not to benefit from her advice, it is the pupil who will suffer as a result. As we have seen, this is likely to happen if the pupil and the teacher inhabit different worlds with different attitudes towards risk and danger. There is something of a clash of cultures, and the result is a lack of communication, an inability of each party to understand the views of the other and a relative ineffectiveness of the teacher's attempts to intervene in the life of the pupil. Teachers have to make the effort to understand the world from the point of view of the pupils, and this means recognizing the nature and extent of their lives as agents. The teachers should not limit themselves to an attempt to control and limit those lives. They need to understand the ways in which the social identities of their pupils are constructed, since then they will be able to demonstrate that they are aware how that social construction takes place.

Young people are unlikely to identify with programmes for promoting safer activities which assume that other people are in control of what they do. Young people cannot always make rational choices between safe and unsafe behaviour. It is not sufficient to provide them with information which helps them make such choices unless this takes account of the specific pressures they may experience as a result of their social and cultural environment. The aim of health education, for example, should be to empower young people to take control of their lives, not to pretend that all they require is the right sort of information. We need to replace a rational choice model of decision-making with one that recognizes the contradictory pressures which govern young people's behaviour. They need to reflect on their experience with the assistance of individuals with whom they can identify, and that reflection should not be regarded as an attempt to control their behaviour by outside forces. On the contrary, it is only likely to be effective if it is seen as empowering them to take control of their lives and point them in the directions they find attractive. But we are not merely concerned with

effectiveness here, since moral issues also arise. We do not want to force
young people to take certain decisions, perhaps because we are successful in frightening them. We want them to see why those decisions are
the right decisions, and how they contribute to the sort of lives which
they wish to lead.

It might be said that if this is right, then it suggests that teachers
are not the right people to do it. We have seen that teachers often have
a very different view of the world as compared with their pupils, and
that the latter do not on the whole identify with their teachers. How,
then, can those teachers effectively intervene in the behaviour of their
pupils? It certainly is true that peer pressure is likely to be far more
influential than teacher pressure in this respect, and if teachers can get
pupils to talk about issues like risk among themselves, this will often
produce ideas and strategies which are likely to benefit them. It could
play a part in an independent active learning activity, in which young
people find out by themselves what the nature of particular activities
are and how they might respond to continuing with those activities in
a safer and more controlled manner. There is evidence that a lot of
young people do this, and their magazines offer suitable advice on how
to develop successful strategies and attitudes in our society when confronted by a variety of possible activities. Sometimes these magazines
do take a rather hectoring line on unsafe behaviour, and their content
is obviously in line with the sorts of fantasies and ambitions their
readers are presumed to have. Yet the agony and advice columns do
provide a good deal of information which can only assist young people
to reflect on their experience, and they even occasionally suggest that
they take a critical attitude to the pressures which society places on
them, even though the features and advertising play a full part in
increasing those pressures in the lives of their readers.

So it is important to see that there is a whole range of influences on
the behaviour and attitudes of young people, and teachers can often
work *with* rather than *against* these sources of information and persuasion. Teachers can play a crucial role in the development of their
pupils' ideas. This is perhaps more through what the teachers do not
do or say than through what they do do. If they portray themselves as
people who know what the answers are, as people whose job it is to
transmit those answers to their pupils, then little progress is likely to be
made. If, on the other hand, they are seen to have views which may
contradict pupils' views, but they nonetheless respect the pupils' views,
then they have created the sort of communicative space in which it is
possible for a variety of views to be compared and assessed. We are not
talking here just about technical means to agreed ends, about which
teachers probably do have more privileged information than their pupils.
We are talking about attitudes to life and death, to risk and loss, and
teachers have no more right to think that their attitudes are correct
than their pupils. By acknowledging this, teachers are in a position to
learn from their pupils in much the same way as the latter can learn
from them. What is involved in such learning? What is learned is that
a certain openness about one's basic attitudes to what constitutes a

valuable human life is appropriate. Then different attitudes can be compared and discussed, and both parties to the discussion can learn a lot about each other and about those attitudes.

This sort of approach may seem to be very unrealistic. It may seem to have little relationship with the experience of communication with pupils which many teachers have. It may look as though what is being suggested here is an ideal form of communication, and one which is unlikely to work in practice. Yet there are schools in which teachers and pupils feel very relaxed together, where they feel that they can discuss issues quite openly and to their mutual benefit. There are teachers who spend a lot of time trying to encourage their pupils to follow the sort of thinking process we represented in Figure 7.1; in other words, to help their pupils reflect on their experience. This is not something which one ever gets entirely right, since it is a complicated and rather obscure process to assess, and what one generally tries to do is create a disposition in the pupil to reflect on his experience and consequent behaviour. What is at issue here is practical reasoning, the application of rationality to our lives, and so it is hardly surprising that it is not a one-off process whereby one is either successful or a failure. Even when we know that we should act in a certain way, we frequently do not, and even more frequently we as teachers and parents fail to construct accurate theories to take account of the consquences of reflection on our experience. Teachers may be older than their pupils, but there is no more reason to think that they are necessarily more sensible than their pupils than there is to think that they are more intelligent than them. Some teachers and some pupils take considerable steps to think carefully about the nature of their actions and experiences, while other teachers and pupils are entirely casual in their attitudes to these areas of their life.

Do the issues related to death have a special role to play here? No doubt most people would agree that it is a good idea for children to be encouraged to reflect upon what they feel and do, but there seems to be a wide range of topics which could prove to be the subject matter of such reflection. This is true, and it is doubtless advantageous to consider those topics too. What is so important about the topics of death, risk and loss is that they represent crucial aspects of our attitude to life itself, and they put teachers and children in a position of equality. This combination is significant. There are other topics which are worth thinking about, certainly, but none which are so central to our conception of ourselves and of what we should be doing. There are other topics which teachers and pupils approach on a more nearly equal basis; for example, general political and moral issues. Yet pupils' relative lack of experience will always put them at a disadvantage when outlining their ideas with their teachers on such issues. These issues have the capacity to appear to be rather abstract and distant from the practical and everyday concerns of people. Only those concepts which are closely connected to death are both central to our lives and not susceptible to 'expert' treatment. There are no experts in these areas, just people who are prepared to consider a range of views they can relate to their own lives and the lives of those connected with them. It is far from ambitious, then, to consider discussing these topics with children. On the contrary, such issues are the most natural and in some ways the easiest things to discuss.

When we think about such discussions, we have emphasized that it is vital that teachers do not just take the attitude that they are involved in trying to prevent their pupils from getting into dangerous activities and lifestyles. Teachers should be in the business of trying to empower young people, to give them the confidence to take control of their own lives and to adopt positive images of themselves. This has an effect upon the teachers too. It can result in teachers also taking a much greater degree of control of their lives as a result of this improved model of communication. Teachers come to appreciate far better the sort of thinking their pupils use, and so gain a vital insight into how the world seems to them. In addition, what pupils tell them gives teachers a lot to think about in relation to their own attitudes. Pupils really have interesting things to say to their teachers, and the latter will have to think about how to reconcile those attitudes to their own thinking. Teachers are then genuinely involved in a dialogue with their pupils, a meeting of attitudes out of which both parties gain. Teachers *and* pupils are empowered through such contact, and this is yet another unique contribution which death as a topic can make to the process of education.

Death education – problems and possibilities

Accepting that death and related issues should be made part of the schooling process is not to answer the question of how to do it. Which teachers will be involved, and in what sort of lesson? Death could come into the curriculum through the ordinary subjects, and teachers could ensure that they spend time discussing those aspects of the ordinary formal curriculum which relate to death and those concepts which are close to it. For example, teachers of literature could spend time looking at accounts of death and loss, and then initiate discussion with pupils about what the latter think of such events. Teachers of art could look at pictures and other representations of death, and ask what they communicate to the viewer, how they relate to the feelings of the pupils themselves. We shall give some details later of such possibilities. On the other hand, there could be a restriction on talking about the topic and it could be limited to specific teachers and to particular areas of the curriculum. Personal and social education comes to mind here, and in many schools it is this area which deals with the topic, in so far as any area does. A third option is for only specific teachers with a trained understanding of the topic to deal with it. This might be considered more appropriate given its capacity to upset children. Those teachers might either seek to respond to the questions which pupils put, or quite generally try to open it up for discussion. They might, on the other hand, restrict themselves to dealing with only those pupils for whom the topic of death and loss is an important issue, perhaps as a result of their personal experiences and history. It would be useful to examine all these alternatives (and of course they are not mutually exclusive) to assess their strengths and weaknesses.

CHAPTER 8

Death, loss and risk as part of the formal curriculum

One can see how these topics could quite easily play a significant role in the formal curriculum. Many subjects in the traditional curriculum do look at issues connected with death, loss and risk. Any subject which examines culture will have to deal at some stage with the views of that culture on these topics. It is very much up to the teacher to decide how to concentrate upon particular aspects of culture, and it is certainly open to her to discuss death and related concepts. Some subjects cannot avoid such discussion. Religious studies is a good example, since it is impossible to understand what a religion is without also understanding what its approach to death is. Religious studies teachers will often explain the differences between religions in terms of their distinct attitudes towards death and loss, and this is as it should be. These topics are clearly crucial aspects of religion and they must be raised in any approach to religion. It is important that teachers present the whole range of alternative views on these topics, even in denominational schools, since otherwise pupils will only have access to a limited number of approaches to the topic. Fortunately, most religions have within them a variety of views to death, so that even if the curriculum is orientated towards a specific faith, it will be possible to raise a number of issues surrounding the topic.

At what stages of the educational process is it suitable to raise such questions? There is a tendency to think that very young children need to be protected from the grimmer aspects of existence, and so it is inappropriate to open such issues up with them. As we have seen, this can be a serious error. Even very young children are interested in issues connected with death, since they will have either direct or indirect experience of death, and they will want to discuss this phenomenon. They will have had pets who have died, relations who have died, and they will have seen people apparently die on the television. They may also be encouraged at school or at home to participate in religious ceremonies which are related to death, especially the death of a co-religionist. Since the topic of death arises quite naturally for such children, it is entirely inappropriate for teachers to avoid it or seek to ignore it. Teachers should try to put aside their personal anxieties regarding this topic and provide a context within which they can discuss it with their pupils in a rewarding manner. When we look at the resources which exist for such teachers, we shall see that there is no shortage of help on this topic for those who are prepared to deal with it.

Junior school teachers have the advantage that they are not so clearly subject teachers as are secondary school teachers, and so it is easier for them to arrange their curriculum around topics. It is not difficult to see how children could be induced to learn a lot about biology, religion, language, history and geography at the same time as they learn about death. Many teachers will seek to organize their teaching around those issues which children find interesting and important anyway, and so it is sensible to use this topic to unify and make more effective the teaching of the curriculum. At the junior stage it is no bad thing to consider topics about which teachers have to admit that they do not have all the answers, since this will encourage pupils to regard their teachers as not necessarily the founts of all knowledge. It is useful for children to discover this early on, since it is likely then that they will realize that they have to take responsibility for their own views from a relatively early stage. They cannot give up that responsibility to adults, and certainly not to teachers. Teachers do know a lot more than their young pupils, yet it is helpful if the latter appreciate that this greater knowledge does not extend over everything. There are some matters about which the children have to make up their own minds, albeit with the assistance and encouragement of their teachers, and the earlier they learn to do this the better. They are thus more likely to develop into critical and reflective individuals, unwilling to allow their autonomy to be submerged under the authority of others.

Not all teachers would enjoy having this sort of relationship with their pupils, of course. Some teachers hate admitting that there are topics on which they are not experts. They may feel that their authority in general would be weakened, even on those topics about which they are expert, and that it would be difficult to preserve discipline if the children do not respect their greater knowledge across the curriculum. Also, they may be teaching in a school which has a denominational allegiance that precludes an entirely open attitude to the topic of death. They may also feel personal anxiety about dealing with a topic which they find upsetting and threatening, and so wonder how successful they would be in bringing it into the curriculum. Finally, they may know or suspect that there are children in their class who would be upset by such a discussion. They may, for example, know that a particular child has just undergone a bereavement experience and is still having problems, and it may strike the teacher as cruel to spend time discussing something which a particular child is likely to regard as directed at himself, and which may upset him further.

These problems raise interesting issues. Should teachers be concerned when issues arise where it is clear that they are no more expert than their pupils? I have argued that this is not a problem, but on the contrary gives teachers an opportunity to get closer to their pupils by acknowledging common difficulties that reflect their shared humanity. One might expect that this would improve the whole context within which teaching and learning takes place. There is no reason to think that such a relationship with pupils would lead to a decline in the authority of the teacher. What would perhaps occur is that pupils would be better able to distinguish between those areas where teachers are experts, and those areas where they are not, and this would only challenge authority if that authority rests on unquestioning obedience to whatever the teacher may say. Teachers should not wish to acquire that sort of authority, for while it may lead to passive and peaceful classrooms, it will seriously get in the way of the child's developing sense of her own autonomy and ability to decide how to behave. It is not desirable to have children who act like automata as a result of their training by teachers in school. We want them to understand the rationale behind the authority which is implicit in the teacher-pupil relationship, and to realize that there are limits to that authority. This is not just a moral point. If we take seriously the notion that we are now living in a postmodern society, the attempt to structure the teacher-pupil relationship along traditional lines according to which all authority comes from above is bound to be futile. The pupils have to find their own route to their future roles in society, and it is natural to expect them to experiment with a variety of roles while still at school. Teachers should help them to work out these roles, not try to impose a particular role on them.

Denominational schools may well expect their teachers to accept that the teaching of their specific religion on death be followed in discussion with the children. That is, after all, one of the points of such schools, to bring children up within the ethos of the religion, and an important part of that ethos is the attitude towards death. Yet in so far as religious education conforms to the process of education as opposed to indoctrination, it will raise a wide series of questions, and will present pupils with a variety of views. Pupils will be encouraged to adopt a particular view, and there will no doubt be much emphasis upon the strength of that view as compared with its competitors, yet it would be vain to try to insulate them from alternative explanations. Most of their pupils live in a secular society where non-religious explanations are widely available, and where different forms of religion are operating, so they will be aware of the non-exclusivity of their own religion's explanation of death. Even if pupils could be presented with only one sort of explanation, there are good educational grounds for thinking that this would be wrong. Part of the educational process involves presenting pupils with a ground-plan of the ideas which are current in our society, and indeed in other societies, and it runs against that process to inculcate in them a particular view so strongly that they cannot even consider the viability of any alternatives. Most teachers of religion would accept this. While they would hope and expect that most of their pupils would find their faith strengthened by the study of their religion in school, teachers would see this as part of the educational aim of increasing children's knowledge and understanding. Underpinning a rational faith is an awareness of how one's own religious commitments differ from those of other people, and to know that, it is necessary to know more than just the principles of one's own faith.

A much more serious difficulty arises when we consider the position of teachers who feel anxious about death, and who as a consequence are very reluctant to discuss it with their pupils. Such teachers may well feel that even though this is a topic worth addressing they themselves are not the right people to do it. We have seen that teachers as an occupational group are in a difficult position here, since they are likely to be especially anxious about death, and if what is required is a calm and relaxed discussion then they are unlikely to be able to organize it. This is an interesting point, and it would clearly be inadvisable to have such teachers lead a discussion on this topic. Not only would they suffer as a result of the experience, but they might be expected to fail to produce the sort of atmosphere in which such a discussion could be of value to the pupils. Those teachers really have to consider what it is about death which particularly worries them and whether it is possible for them to change over time in order to carry out that sort of work. A female teacher of 9-year-olds in north London reported that:

> I did feel that we ought to talk seriously about what happens when people die . . . we had just visited some mummies in the British Museum, and when we got back to school all the children wanted to talk about it. They kept on asking where the dead people had gone, what happens when we die, and so on. I didn't know what to say, and my hands went clammy and I started to sweat, because I really don't like talking about death and things like that.

This is a far from untypical reaction. Surely we could not expect such teachers to initiate and develop a discussion with their pupils on the topic?

What we might expect is that a teacher who finds herself in this position would take steps to come to terms with her attitude to the subject. That does not mean that she should suddenly face up to it, since that would probably not be possible anyway. What is required is an acknowledgement that this is an important issue on which children have the right to expect their teacher to comment. I have also argued that it is a topic which can bring great benefits to the teacher-pupil relationship, since it can lead to an overcoming of the barriers which often separate them. This is not a problem which relates exclusively to death, as there are a number of issues which may embarrass or worry a teacher, and yet where we might hope that they would try to put their personal qualms to one side for the sake of the education of their pupils. The first step is for the teacher to acknowledge that there are issues which concern her, and for her to work out ways in which she can become more relaxed in presenting them to children. There are things which professionals on occasion do not wish to do, but do because they understand that it is an important part of their job. It is interesting that in the case of the teacher just quoted we see an admission that she should have been able to raise the issue of death with the children, since they were interested in raising it with her. One reason for taking them to see the mummies was to explore different cultural and historical approaches to death, and it is a great help to the pupils' learning if the teacher can relate what they experience in the museum to wider and more personal topics. She herself felt that she ought to be able to do this, but at that moment she also felt unable to do so. Such an attitude should not be treated as final, but as a problem to be overcome.

The last problem is that there may be children in the class who have had a recent bereavement experience which makes them very sensitive about the topic, and the teacher may as a consequence be reluctant to raise it. Those children may feel that they are being picked out in what is being said about death, and they may resent such treatment. What is important about this sort of case is the understanding which the teacher has of his class. It would be wrong to spend a lot of time talking about anything which is likely to upset the children, and we have to assume that the teacher will know what his children would find upsetting. It is not necessarily the case that children will find death upsetting, and many children, especially very young ones, take a very practical attitude towards death. They are happy to talk about it, about their feelings at the time and what happened, and they are perfectly prepared to share their experiences with their classmates. Adults may react with some surprise, and indeed horror, at the apparently easy way in which many young children can accommodate death within their view of the world and of their own future. If that is the attitude which recently bereaved children have to death, then it can quite easily form part of a discussion in the class, and those children will have interesting and rewarding comments to make to the class as a whole. They should certainly not be forced to talk to the class unless they wish to do so, but if they do, then they can produce a fund of ideas and advice which will be a very useful resource for the class as a whole.

Yet there may be children in the class who have had especially bad bereavement experiences, or who for some other reason strongly wish to avoid the topic. Would it be acceptable for teachers to force them to confront a topic to which they are so antagonistic? One might take the muscular view that it *is* acceptable, since this is an important topic and children must spend some time in school thinking about it. This would be an inappropriate strategy. Even if we could justify trampling on the individual child's sensibilities, which is doubtful, it is hardly likely to be very effective. If a child is determined to avoid a topic because she regards it as upsetting, then she will find it even more upsetting if she is forced to confront it. Her negative feelings about the topic will be magnified, not reduced, and the whole point of raising the topic will be lost. When we look at the context within which a teacher contemplates raising difficult issues with children, we have to rely upon the professional knowledge which the teacher has of the class and the personal knowledge which he has of the individuals in the class. There is a tendency for teachers to think that what would upset them would upset children, but we have to assume here that it is possible for teachers to be sufficiently detached from their personal anxieties to gain an accurate view of the feelings of their class. Often teachers are justified in thinking that raising a certain issue would cause at least some pupils to suffer anxiety.

Let us look at an example. A male teacher of 6-year-olds had a boy in his class who was experiencing a variety of learning problems as a result of the emotional disturbance caused by his mother's death. She was, in fact, murdered in front of him by her husband – his father. The child was not paying attention in most of his lessons, and his behaviour was erratic, sometimes very aggressive and at other times rather withdrawn. The other children in the school tended to pick on him, and they had no compunction about reminding him frequently of the recent tragic circumstances in his home. His teacher was eager to discuss with the class as a whole some of the issues relating to death which I have mentioned in this book, especially the dangers associated with some of the practices which were popular with the children. Yet he felt constrained by the presence of this particular child from explaining in detail what was involved in being killed violently, since he expected (surely with some justification) that it would especially upset that child. He also wanted to talk to the children about the tragic events in that child's life, to try to persuade them not to persecute him. So the teacher was in a dilemma. He thought that if he could discuss death with the children he could help the child get on with his schoolmates, and also prevent some of the children at least from coming to a violent end themselves. On the other hand, he did not want to add to that child's problems by discussing those topics, however obliquely, with him present.

As it happened, he got around these problems quite simply. He waited until the child was absent one day from school, and then he spoke to the other children quite frankly about the events which had led up to the murder. The children talked about what is involved in a murder, and what it would be like to have a parent murdered, and for the murderer to be the other parent. The children reacted in a practical way, asking who would then look after the survivor and what it would feel like to be in that sort of situation. The teacher was able to discuss the phenomenon of death in general, and to point out to them that some of the activities in the locality which even very young children could be drawn into were potentially dangerous and could lead to their own deaths. He emphasized the dangers of doing what they were told to do by older children, and he encouraged them to think about their own deaths and the effect that it would have on others. It was noticeable after this session that the bereaved child had an easier time of it in the school, and the teacher followed this discussion up with renewed discussions whenever that child was absent. His classmates came to understand far better what he had experienced and why his behaviour was sometimes difficult. They also started to grasp the true nature of some of the activities which went on in their neighbourhood, and became more aware of their links with death and injury. It would be wrong to suggest that as a result all was sweetness and light, but there was a definite improvement in the treatment of the bereaved child and also in the out-of-school behaviour of the other children.

The important point to make about introducing the topic of death into the curriculum is that it should be done in response to the questions which children quite naturally ask. It should not be imposed on unwilling and nervous pupils, and no attempt should be made to discuss anything with them which they will find disturbing unless it concerns an issue which they themselves have identified as relevant to their lives. There certainly would be moral problems about undertaking to raise a subject with children which could reasonably be expected to upset them, although some teachers would argue that the benefits of the 'shock treatment' might be greater than the harm. This is a dangerous argument to offer. It goes far beyond the role of the teacher to try to change the behaviour of a pupil by shocking him, although what actually transpires in a lesson may shock him. This is not an effect which a teacher can directly try to produce without usurping the role of the parents or the family of that child. They have a right to be consulted if teachers wish to affect the emotions of their children in a direct way, since the family may well have views on what would be an appropriate topic for their children.

Let us look at an example here. Many children were strongly affected by the film *Schindler's List*, which they found to be upsetting. It was not just a horror film, though, but a film which presented the actual events as they occurred to many victims during the dominance of Nazi Germany in Europe. This was a film which young people attended outside of school, but they often wanted to discuss it in school, and some teachers showed other material which displayed some of the horrors of concentration camp life. A parent came subsequently to the headteacher to complain that his daughter had experienced nightmares and appeared to be generally unhappy after seeing this sort of material. He blamed the school for this and said it should be stopped. He argued that it was not the role of the school to upset his child, and that if he wanted to confront his child with the sort of pictures of dead bodies and gas chambers which the school had shown her, then he would organize it himself. He expressed his view that it was the job of the school to educate his child, not terrify her, and his argument was that the school should stick to the formal curriculum and to the basics of education.

What was interesting about this confrontation was that he had raised an important point. How far can the school allow itself to play on the emotions of its pupils? The angry parent did not understand that the Holocaust is actually part of the formal curriculum, but this does not really invalidate his argument, since the main object of his criticism was the very graphic way in which images of the Holocaust were presented to the children. The school had a good argument in response. The headteacher pointed out that this topic was part of the National Curriculum, and that teachers do more than just talk, write on the blackboard and refer to textbooks. There is an increasing use of the media in schools to help illustrate elements of the curriculum, since pupils will often learn more effectively if they can see filmed material on videos, or if they are presented with vivid pictorial representations of the topic under discussion. There obviously are instances when pupils become unduly affected by this sort of material, and there is nothing wrong with that. The point of using vivid images is to engage their emotions, to make what they are seeing more real to them. As a result the pupils are in a better position to understand how the historical event was experienced by the participants, which is a useful means of gaining understanding.

If it is acceptable to use dramatic images to attract the interest and commitment of the pupils, then there will be occasions when pupils become very involved emotionally in the topic being discussed. Some pupils will be unhappy as a result of that involvement, and one might wonder whether that is acceptable as part of the compulsory curriculum. It could be argued that it is acceptable, but only as an indirect consequence of what takes place within the curriculum. That is, teachers may acknowledge that what they are presenting to children may upset some of them, but they should not go out of their way to obtain this result. If teachers are to avoid anything which might upset children, then they would have to abandon a great deal of the curriculum. Many apparently innocuous passages in novels, for example, are capable of upsetting some children, as are aspects of history, biology and science in general. Anything may be felt by a particular pupil to have a resonance for him which is threatening and disturbing. It is very much up to the professionalism of the teacher to work out how to present potentially upsetting material to her class in ways which will maximize learning and minimize anxiety.

We cannot emphasize sufficiently the role of the teacher in understanding her class and knowing how to present a topic in a way which will not aggravate individual problems which certain pupils have with that topic, or an aspect of it. Most teachers in junior schools will have a good knowledge of their pupils, and they will understand how difficult issues should be raised and developed. It may be that they will do this when some of the children are not there, in order to avoid upsetting them any further where they are already in a particularly difficult position. It may be that the class will be split up into different groups and the topic presented in ways which are appropriate to each specific group. Teachers in junior schools generally have a fairly good understanding of each individual child, and should be able to interpret the curriculum in a way that respects the sensitivities of particular pupils. The position in secondary schools is rather different, since teachers might have less contact with children and so know less about them. Of course, the older the pupils, the more responsibility they should take for their own response to the curriculum, but this does not mean that teachers no longer have to be aware of the potential emotional difficulties which the curriculum has for pupils. What the teacher should do is use her understanding of the pupils to try to alleviate individual anxieties, while at the same time persevering with the curriculum with the aim of discussing difficult issues with all the pupils. If we were contemplating discussing trivial but upsetting issues with pupils there would be no problem, since such issues could just be excluded. However, issues which are trivial would be uncontroversial, since they would not be capable of producing anxiety among the pupils. What we are dealing with here are issues which are universal and crucial, and any consequent anxiety among pupils has to be regarded as a price worth paying for allowing such issues into the curriculum.

If death and related issues should be dealt with in school, then there are good arguments for bringing them explicitly into the formal curriculum. Learning is likely to be more effective if it is felt to be relevant by pupils to their lives, and few topics are capable of arousing the interest of pupils in the way that death and risk can. Themes which run right through the formal curriculum can help to unify that curriculum, so that pupils do not think of what they are doing as a random collection of subjects and topics. If pupils can recognize that there are certain themes which much of the curriculum debates, then they will be better able to realize that the curriculum is integrated. This might also be expected to aid learning, since pupils will see that there is a pattern to the different areas of knowledge with which they are confronted, and thus they can to a degree grasp its structure as a whole. It becomes less mysterious to them why they are dealing with so many different forms of knowledge, each with its own distinct methodology and subject matter.

How might this be done? Suppose a school decided to look at death as a cross-curricular theme, and so wondered how it might be made part of the formal curriculum. Teachers of English and foreign language literature could look at the ways in which writers had dealt with the topic, concentrating perhaps on the treatment in the set books they are using in the school syllabus. They could discuss death-bed scenes, accounts of funerals, reactions to loss, mourning rituals, images of war and conflict, descriptions of risky behaviour, attitudes to health, and so on. Books from earlier periods often have descriptions of actions and rituals which contrast nicely with more modern aspects of death, and the contrast could be discussed and developed in the classroom. Contrasts between practices in different countries can be outlined in geography and foreign-language lessons. There is a lot of scope for religious studies to continue with this sort of topic, through an investigation of the different approaches of different religious faiths. These can be related to the communities which practise those faiths, and pupils can then compare the variety of beliefs and practices with those with which they are familiar. Science can examine the physical processes of death and injury, and the ways in which matter can be degraded, and physical education can explore aspects of physical risk. It would of course be necessary for teachers in the school to get together and work out how they were going to present the topic, so that it came over to the pupils as an integrated discussion rather than a random series of observations, but this could be a very time-consuming process. It is always difficult to get teachers to plan across the curriculum in this sort of way, and if they can be convinced that it is feasible without long and frequent meetings they are more likely to feel able to undertake it. Virtually every curriculum area could be included in the development of such cross-curricular work without requiring an enormous amount of time and effort on behalf of the individual teachers, and there are advantages in doing so which are over and above the benefits of addressing this topic.

What are these advantages? They relate to the way the curriculum is delivered. Far too often teachers have little or no idea what other teachers in other subject areas are doing, and many teachers snipe at their colleagues and the subjects they teach. While this can often be harmless and lighthearted, it can reveal a hiatus in the delivery of the curriculum which is potentially harmful to the learning of the pupils. Teachers will often behave as though they are in competition with each other, and within such an atmosphere cooperation becomes difficult and strained. If teachers can agree that a particular topic is so important that it is worth thinking carefully about how it is presented, and how the different areas of the curriculum can get together to produce the most effective treatment of that topic, then this is going to have valuable side-effects for the rest of the curriculum. Teachers will find it easier to talk to each other in general about their work, and they will think more carefully about the way what they do is reflected and organized in other departments and subject areas. Thinking in this way will help unify the curriculum, making it more perspicuous to the children. This is likely to have significant benefits for pupils, who will see that the school curriculum presents a variety of perspectives on common issues. This may be very different from their general attitude to that curriculum, and anything which will help them regard the curriculum as a whole could also help them find their way about it more easily.

Much of this is true of any theme which is taken to run through the curriculum. It could be equal opportunities, for example, or health education. But death, and related topics, have an important characteristic which is not shared by all comparable themes, namely, the universality and centrality of the issue. It deals with questions which children quite readily wish to ask, and it relates to their immediate concerns. If it is incorporated in the formal curriculum, the school will be seen to be responding to the needs and interests of its pupils in a clear and direct way, thereby helping them link their personal lives to the curriculum itself. Normally that link is only visible to teachers, and if it can be communicated to children it will encourage them to regard what goes on in the formal curriculum as part of their lives, not a distant set of activities which are imposed on them. When we talk about using death as a cross-curricular theme we do not mean that pupils will spend most of their time contemplating skulls or reading about different mourning customs in diverse communities. They would only spend a relatively small amount of time on these and related topics, and the latter would be used to give the curriculum a focus which otherwise it might not be seen to have. Pupils would get used to the idea that it is necessary to take an objective view of death and related issues, since the formal curriculum is itself all about objectivity and rational explanation. It follows that they are then in a position to take control of these issues, as opposed to having the issues take control of them. The benefits of such a development in education are not hard to imagine.

CHAPTER 9

Should teaching about death be limited?

We have looked at some of the possibilities that arise when we consider how the formal curriculum might respond to the introduction of death and related concepts. I have concentrated on the advantages of such a development in the curriculum, although the problems have also been acknowledged. There are always difficulties in introducing new organizing principles into the formal curriculum, and it is commonplace for educational theorists to pay insufficient attention to the practical difficulties of innovation. The sort of examples we were considering, though, did not call for a major reorganization of the curriculum, but more a reorganization of the way part of it, and it could be quite a small part, is delivered. It might be felt, though, that this particular network of concepts centring on death is too sensitive to be taught by just any teacher in any subject area. We have already seen that some children may be upset by what they have experienced outside school, and do not enjoy being reminded of those experiences while doing history or physical education, for instance. We have also looked at the problems which teachers may feel they have in confronting difficult topics such as death. They may wonder whether they are properly equipped to deal with the topic, or whether it would be better belonging to a specific part of the curriculum, where it is taught by teachers who specialize in that area.

There certainly is a role in schools for teachers who have specific counselling skills which enable them to help children with any personal problems they might have. It should not be expected of just any teacher that she could deal successfully with a difficult personal problem, or even that she would wish to undertake this sort of activity. While most teachers are concerned for the emotional and physical wellbeing of their pupils, the expertise of these teachers is surely limited, and they would be cautious before entering into the attempted resolution of what pupils regard as their problems. This is not something which anyone can undertake lightly without threatening her professional integrity. Although it is to be hoped that all teachers will have some insight into how the world is seen from the point of view of their pupils, this is not much of a starting point for resolving their problems. Indeed, one might go further and point out that a teacher may have an excellent grasp of an individual pupil's problems, and yet have no idea how those problems might be resolved. The sort of expertise which is in question here is not necessarily part of the professional armoury of each and every teacher. If it were, there would presumably be no need for the courses that exist to help teachers acquire the skills necessary to address the problems of their pupils.

Yet even if one assumes that specific counselling skills are limited to just a few teachers, it does not follow that those teachers should be the exclusive founts of information on death. For one thing, children may have a successful relationship with certain teachers, and it would be unfortunate were those teachers to feel unable to deal with those children's problems just because they were not officially designated as the appropriate teachers for the task, or because they had not success-fully completed a course on how to deal with pupils' problems. It is not easy to get children to discuss what is worrying them with their teachers, and when the occasion arises it has to be dealt with there and then, not put on the backburner to be raised on another occasion. That future occasion may never arise, and the child may not feel at ease with a different teacher. There are certain quite natural contexts within which such issues arise, and it would be a shame were the teacher to have to refer the pupil to someone else. What is often important is the way a problem is made available to a certain teacher, not because he is the best person to resolve the problem, but because he is the best person to listen to the problem in the opinion of the pupil.

But it will be argued that if a disturbed child goes to a teacher who in fact understands very little of what the child is undergoing, then the teacher can do more harm than good. When we consider issues such as death, loss and risk we are considering very important issues in the life and character-development of a pupil, and he needs to come into contact with a teacher who has a knowledgeable and perceptive grasp of the situation, including a lot of information about how children deal with these matters. A teacher who is not able to understand the situation fully is going to be more of a liability than an aid to the pupil. This is not necessarily the case. Often children will relate far better to teachers who may have only a vague interest and understanding of their prob-lems. For example, I spoke to a 12-year-old boy whose mother was HIV positive and who was worried about what was going to happen in the future when she became ill and eventually died. The school was aware of the situation but the other children in the school, apart from one very close friend, were not. The boy was also worried about what would happen to him after his mother, his only remaining parent, died, and quite clearly felt guilty that he was concerned about his own wellbeing in such a situation. Much to the surprise of all the staff, the teacher with whom he spent most time talking about it was the physical edu-cation teacher, a bluff and curt middle-aged man. What he appreciated in talking to this teacher was that he got hardly any response, according to the pupil, and the teacher did nothing more than listen. This impressed the boy, since the self-reliance of the adult contrasted so sharply with his own feelings of doubt and weakness, and he felt that he could imbibe something of the tough attitude of the adult towards life just by being in his presence. The teachers who were interested in talking with him about his situation he rejected, despite what they regarded their skills as counsellors to be. He rejected them precisely because of their attempts at being open to his experiences. He wanted exactly the opposite, an image of resolution and strength, a symbol of action without too much prior thought.

Pupils relate to different teachers in different ways. They realize that different teachers are useful for different things, and when a child is undergoing some emotional difficulty, she can often be relied upon to select the right person to come to and discuss it. For such a discussion to work, it is not necessary that the teacher actually do or say anything. He certainly does not have to relate to the topic which the child wishes to raise, since there is frequently a roundabout conversation which never directly makes contact with the problem. What can be more important than what is said is what remains unsaid, the sympathy which the pupil may feel is possessed by the teacher. A 16-year-old girl who was about to take her GCSE in French was experiencing a lot of problems in coping with a boyfriend who wanted to have unprotected sex with her. She was considering it seriously, since although she recognized the risks involved she wanted to hold on to him. She did not feel that she could discuss the situation with anyone in the school, and certainly not directly with any of the teachers. She had a good relationship with her French teacher, whom she regarded as strong and independent. She went to discuss a grammatical point with this teacher, something which she had never quite managed to understand in class, but what was uppermost in her mind was her dilemma.

It is interesting to see how the conversation went, according to the girl. She reported:

> I stayed on after the lesson and asked Miss to explain the use of 'y' in French, which is one of those things I have never quite managed to grasp . . . and we were talking about it, but I wasn't concentrating on it that much, 'cos I was thinking about John, and then I looked at her and thought, well, would she be pushed into doing something she didn't want to do, and I don't think she would, really. It's the same as the use of 'y' in French, there are rules and you've got to stick with them, and you cannot change them however much you'd like to. When she was telling me the rules of 'y' it was like she was saying 'This is what you've got to do if you're going to speak French', and I thought to myself, 'This is what I've got to do if I'm going to be able to make my own decisions.' So although we were talking about one thing, we were really talking about something else as well, and when I saw John next I told him that I had made my mind up definitely and I wasn't going to take the risk.

The teacher had helped her come to terms with risk without her even knowing what she had done. Had the teacher asked the girl a direct question about the topic of risk she would have been very unlikely to receive a straight answer, or any answer at all. Had the girl had to rely for advice on specific members of staff in the school she would never have gone near them. This apparently casual conversation on an entirely different topic proved decisive in this case.

It might be thought that what had proved to be helpful in this case was not the relationship between the pupil and the teacher, but a purely arbitrary association of ideas which the pupil had made. After all, she had not gone to the teacher for advice, and it seems entirely coincidental that what occurred led her to take a certain decision. I would not want to suggest either that the decision in this case was the right decision, but it was right in the sense that it was the conclusion to a period of thinking and reflection on the part of the individual. She came to a decision about what her attitude to this type of risk was going to be, and she could have come to a different decision. As we have seen, there is no entirely objective standard of risk which specifies what levels of risk are acceptable or otherwise, and so she might quite properly have felt that the risk of losing her boyfriend was more significant than the risk of HIV infection or becoming pregnant. Her reflection on the conversation with the teacher could have led her in quite the opposite direction as far as the actual decision went. What is important about her decision is that it is something which she has considered and not just made out of impulse or as a reaction to the pressure of others. It does seem rather haphazard, though, if a pupil has to rely on an encounter with a teacher which takes this sort of indeterminate form for it to be possible to reflect upon the pupil's feelings and future behaviour. Surely it would be far better for the pupils to be able to go to particular teachers who are trained to help them when they have difficulties and work with them on resolving those difficulties.

It certainly is very useful if a school has such teachers, but we should not assume that pupils will necessarily want to go to them or that they would choose them over the teachers with whom they feel more at ease. We have seen how many bereaved children complain about the way in which they felt counsellors tried to direct their grief along a path which the counsellors themselves thought was normal. Many of these children were of the opinion that instead of being helped by the counsellors, they were 'taken over' by them and had to pretend to agree that their feelings were in accord with the counsellors' wishes. Even if counsellors do not do this, they may not be the people with whom young people wish to work. There is a lot to be said for thinking of the teachers with whom they are familiar as a useful resource in coming to terms with their difficulties. After all, pupils may have a long experience of working with particular teachers, and it is not unlikely that by the time they require emotional support they themselves know very well which teachers are going to be helpful and which are not. We should not underestimate the ability of children to take appropriate practical steps to resolve their own problems in efficient and direct ways. This may involve going to counsellors, or teachers with an understanding of counselling, or it may involve going to entirely different teachers altogether, those teachers whom they know and whom they feel know them.

There is, of course, an area of the curriculum called Personal and Social Education which might be expected to touch on issues connected with death. Teachers who work in this area might be expected to have the expertise to raise relevant questions with children in a non-threatening and productive way, and one might suggest that such questions should be restricted to this area of the curriculum. Teachers of Personal and Social Education (PSE) or its equivalent have a good understanding of how to tackle problems which pupils may be having, and how to anticipate such problems. Even in junior schools teachers frequently set aside part of the curriculum to deal with issues which arise formally as part of PSE in the secondary school. Some of these issues will relate to death. Teachers will certainly talk about risk and health, they may even mention death directly, and they will often consider the notion of loss. They will want to ensure that these topics are covered to some degree in the class, since otherwise the only information which pupils may have could be very limited or non-existent. In junior schools teachers will generally integrate the topic with something else they are studying, so that a visit to a wood, for example, may lead to a discussion of some of the dead animals which are to be seen, and which may be related to the children themselves and to human beings in general. A lesson which looks at aspects of the body may consider ageing and death, and discuss the vital organs in the body. In these sorts of ways teachers can introduce quite complex notions gradually and in a way which makes sense to the child. This sort of approach has the advantage that it integrates what is done on death and related concepts with the rest of the curriculum, so that these topics arise in what seems to be an entirely natural way. It may not, in fact, be quite so natural, since the teacher may well have thought through quite precisely how and exactly when she is going to raise these issues, but it can be expected to be far less potentially threatening for the child if questions about death seem to emerge out of other questions.

One of the features of teaching in junior schools which strikes any new teacher is the wide frame of reference which children apply to what they learn. They ask very broad questions about what the teacher tells them, and they are often interested in entirely tangential issues. These have struck a chord somewhere with a particular child, and she wants an answer to a question which the teacher may not ever have considered to be related to the topic under discussion. Teachers can use this both to extend the understanding and verbal fluency of the children, and also to make a connection with what interests them. When children start talking about issues related to death the discussion frequently roams all over the place, since the child's view of the network of concepts related to death may be very different from that of the teacher. What sometimes happens with teachers who are themselves very anxious about death is that they tend to try to restrict this wandering around the topic. This can be a shame, since pupils use this apparently casual approach to the topic to reveal issues which interest them and which require development. If they are allowed to work in this sort of way they can increase their sense of their own self-esteem and the ability of the school to relate to their own interests.

It might be worth taking a look at an example of a visit by a class of 6-year-olds in the Midlands to a museum which had Egyptian mummies in it. The lesson was supposed to be about how the Egyptians lived, and the children were taught something about hieroglyphics and the sort of paintings which Egyptian culture produced. But most of them were really interested in the mummies, especially the fact that they were for the first time actually looking at dead people. In this museum there was only one mummy on view, but lots of sarcophagi which the children thought contained mummies. This gave rise to a lot of questions about death, which the teacher quite strenuously avoided:

John: Why did they wrap their dead people up in bandages, Miss?
Teacher: They did that because they thought that the dead would wake up and carry on living in the next world with the things which they had with them in their coffins.
Theresa: Is that what really happens, Miss?
Teacher: No, well it doesn't really happen, but that's what they thought.
John: My gran says that after you're dead you either go to hell or heaven.
Teacher: Yes, well, the Egyptians did not really believe that.
Jenny: When my father died I don't think he was wrapped up like that.
Teacher: That's because he didn't live in ancient Egypt.
Jenny: Well, where did he go then? Did he have anything to take with him in the earth?
Teacher: I don't know, Jenny, I don't think he did.
Jenny: If he didn't have anything with him, he couldn't do anything when he wakes up, could he, Miss?
Teacher: We're getting away from the point here, we're supposed to be talking about the ancient Egyptians.
John: I wish I had a mummy at home, Miss, could we get one?
Joe: If I had a mummy at home, it could help my mum with the housework.
Teacher: Now you're being silly. Let's get back to looking at the paintings on the lid of the thing the mummies are put in.

The children constantly tried to extend the discussion to areas of enquiry which interested them, and the teacher just as constantly tried to steer it back to the narrow topic which she had in mind. To a degree this resulted in the topic becoming of less direct concern to them, since instead of it relating to issues which they wished to explore, she insisted that it be limited to issues which she wished to explore, issues which are quite separate from the lives of children. Some lessons on Egyptian mummies take a very different route. Some teachers will demonstrate with a child lying prone on a table the process by which the internal organs of the corpse were extracted, and will then talk about how the body decays and the ways in which the mummification process slowed this down. Some teachers will use this to talk about death and decay, and also about different views of the afterlife. This has the advantage of relating the topic to what is familiar to the children, what they hear talked about at home and on the television, and what they might have personal knowledge of. They are more likely under such circumstances to be able to connect their work in school with real issues outside school, and so improve not only their attitude to their school work but also see it as useful for dealing with real practical issues.

The advantage of connecting this sort of discussion to a particular topic is that it helps the child take up an objective attitude to issues which are in themselves highly subjective. One's attitude to death, for example, is something which develops over time and can take a number of different forms, reflecting the personality and experiences of the individual. Through being able to connect attitude to an area of objective knowledge, in this case to the customs of the ancient Egyptians, one is better able to view that attitude from an objective standpoint, as just one attitude among many competing attitudes, and it can then be assessed and reflected upon. Even schools which favour a particular religious answer to issues related to death will introduce pupils to a variety of views through their understanding of different cultures and historical periods. Ideally this will enable the child to stand back from his particular situation and evaluate his approach. This is particularly important when it comes to looking at issues which are surrounded by emotions, and which it is not easy to detach from one's own way of acting. This will not happen instantaneously. It takes a lot of time and practice before one can acquire this sort of control over one's attitudes and emotions. If it can ever come about, it is going to have to start when children are young and beginning to form their ideas of themselves and their world.

What is at issue here is not the school trying to mould the child in a particular form, which obviously would be undesirable unless what was being done was publicly discussed and complied with the wishes of the parents. The school is in a position to respond to the natural questions of its pupils in a way which can help those children take control of their own lives. This should not be seen as a process which has an obvious start or a perceptible conclusion, but it extends over our entire lives. In so far as we can relate what is happening to us to a broader structure of events, we are in a position to stand back and consider what we are feeling and what we are going to do from a more objective standpoint. One of the social traits which schools try to cultivate is the ability to think about what one is doing before one does it, to prevent children from growing up into the sort of people who just react to events without thinking about what they are doing or what the consequences of that action might be for others. Some of the topics which teachers use to try to inculcate such moral virtues are trivial and are rightly regarded as such by the pupils. A marked advantage of talking about some of the issues connected with death is that they are obviously not trivial, and they immediately engage the interest of most children. They touch on questions and ideas which the children themselves have already considered, and on the whole they are eager to discuss those opinions with others.

One of the advantages of introducing topics such as death in the junior school is that the structure of teaching and learning is often fluid enough to make it easy to talk around a topic in an unforced way. Children may well be encouraged to relate different areas of the curriculum by concentrating upon a particular topic, and many teachers will encourage children to work out the wider implications of what they are studying. There is a danger in this, in that important ideas which are worth raising within the classroom may be omitted because the teacher has not sought to include those ideas, and has on the contrary taken direct steps to avoid them. Yet all teachers will see it as desirable that their pupils be given the tools to enable them to be autonomous agents, and these are just as much personal as they are academic and physical. All teachers will be concerned about the personal safety of their pupils and so will need to raise with them the topic of risk and taking care of themselves in potentially dangerous situations. All teachers, therefore, will welcome the opportunity to introduce into their work with pupils ideas connected with the topic of death, if they can be convinced that it is possible to do so without provoking anxieties in the children, and indeed in the teachers themselves. We have seen throughout this discussion that there are good arguments for making the effort.

It is becoming evident, I hope, that it is not necessarily a good idea in the junior school to have important issues discussed in special sessions devoted just to them. It is far better to relate the issues to the normal curriculum, and to respond to the questions children will produce regarding those issues when they arise. The situation is different in the secondary school, where there is a specific area of the curriculum devoted to topics like death – Personal and Social Education – with specialist teachers who are there to deal with those topics. One might have thought that death would be an important topic in PSE, but there is little evidence that it is. The topic does not figure greatly in the syllabi which exist at the moment, and as we have seen this may be largely due to the disinclination of teachers to deal with it, and the idea that it is too gloomy a topic for children. One 15-year-old boy told me that he thought having a series of lessons on the dangers of drug abuse without also talking about death is like seeing *Hamlet* without the ghost. This is not to suggest that death is the only or even the main topic which should occur in PSE. That would be a ridiculous suggestion. Even talking about drug abuse has many facets which have nothing to do with death, and a teacher would discuss a whole range of issues with references to drugs, not just the possible final consequences of their abuse.

One of the advantages of talking about death in such a context is that it brings out the seriousness of the activity, and encourages the pupil to consider his attitude to what might well be a consequence of his actions. One of the disadvantages of talking about death in such a lesson is that the pupils may well have no experience of anyone who has died as a result of the activities being discussed, while they would have experience of people who have suffered other consequences. For example, given the long period from the acquisition of HIV to the development of AIDS and eventual death, it is hardly likely to play a part in the experience of most teenagers. So when one is talking about unprotected sex it might be more sensible to talk about the dangers of pregnancy and sexually transmitted diseases (the less serious varieties), since these are topics about which pupils may well have personal experience. They could easily know people who had become pregnant by a chance sexual encounter or who had acquired a sexually transmitted disease, and so what the teacher is saying to them connects with their experience. It is surely sensible to concentrate upon an existing aspect of pupils' understanding of the topic rather than to relate it to a notion which is quite distant from that understanding.

There is another danger in emphasizing the life-and-death significance of what the pupils might be tempted to do, and this lies in glamorizing those activities. We have seen that young people may have a very different attitude to their future compared with their teachers, and they may be tempted by an activity if they are told that it is potentially dangerous. I remember seeing a lesson on the perils of glue sniffing, which ended with some graphic pictures of young people whose bodies had swollen up and turned black on death. The teacher obviously expected his audience to be horrified by these pictures, and some of them certainly were, but whether these children would ever have been tempted to sniff glue struck me as questionable. A group of boys who quite happily admitted that they knew people who did sniff glue, and who had, the teacher suspected, participated in the activity, were not apparently put off by these pictures. On the contrary, they obviously thought that it added to the excitement of the activity. They had never seen anyone they knew die of it, although they did know that one could die, and they thought that the gruesomeness of the deaths they saw was rather intriguing.

Of course, one is never quite sure what the real impression such images have on children is. The bravado of a public occasion can easily be replaced by more searching attitudes in private. Yet there is no reason to think that young people, especially young men, will find themselves put off by images of death and injury. One important issue here is that it is very different to show someone an image of death from getting him to think of himself as being in that situation. As we have seen, many young people find it difficult to imagine themselves dead, and so do not really feel that the images of death with which they are sometimes confronted have anything to do with them. The problem which many young people have in PSE is that they feel they are being provided with information designed to persuade them to behave in particular ways, and yet they are not provided with the means to empathize with the examples which their teachers offer. It is not enough to present an image of someone who has died, or suffered, or is unwell as a result of her behaviour in order for young people to make the connection. The connection may be obvious to the teacher, but it can remain obscure to the pupil. One reason why this is so is because the teacher and the pupil may have a very different view of the world from each other, and there is not sufficient mutual agreement on what such images mean for the point which the teacher wishes to make to carry over to the pupils. They may be able to acknowledge the relevance of the point rationally, but not emotionally, and this is surely a serious omission.

What has to happen in order for pupils to derive the same meanings from the images of death and illness as their teachers? There has to be some understanding of the ways pupils view the world, and they should be encouraged to make the mental effort to see the world from the teacher's point of view. Although we live in a common culture, it is an error to think that we interpret images in the same way regardless of our position in that culture, and the ways different people interpret such messages is an important subject for PSE. Perhaps the most important idea which PSE teachers wish to get across is that what they are talking about relates to the pupils. It is not a distant and abstract account of people's lives somewhere else, but is of direct relevance to pupils' own lives. One thing which often gets in the way of such an idea is the feeling by many pupils that teachers are trying to get them to behave in certain ways, ways which teachers regard as prudent but which may go against the sort of view of the world which young people themselves accept. In just the same way that pupils try to resist the formal curriculum which is broken down into subjects, they may also seek to resist the imposition of the ideas of PSE. These ideas may be as alien to them as the values implicit in the rest of the curriculum. It is the task of the PSE teacher to make these ideas real to pupils, so that they can realistically use them when considering how they are to act.

Often this does not take place. The teacher produces what she thinks is a strong case against a certain course of action, and illustrates her account powerfully with graphic images and reports from young people. Instead of being impressed by this, some young people seem oblivious to the message she is trying to convey. A natural reaction by the teacher in such a situation is to doubt the ability of her pupils to understand what it is to act in their own self-interest, which may result in a lack of enthusiasm on her part in convincing the pupils of the relevance of what she is teaching for their lives and wellbeing. It is uninspiring to be teaching something which many of one's pupils quite blatantly reject. Of course, this rejection may not primarily be of the topic nor of the teacher, but of the schooling system itself, and pupils may wish to oppose that system by resisting aspects of the curriculum which otherwise they would find both relevant and interesting. It has to be admitted, though, that much of the PSE curriculum is difficult to deliver convincingly if a sizeable section of the class is disinclined to participate in the process. Such a lack of enthusiasm on the part of pupils may have its source in another area of the school curriculum, or in schooling itself, and it is hardly a fair criticism of the PSE teacher if pupils use her class as an arena for expressing their hostility to other aspects of the school. Given the relatively informal nature of much PSE teaching, it represents something of a perfect opportunity for children to express their general disapproval of school, or indeed of even wider institutions such as society.

There are ways in which the PSE teacher can fight back. She can seek to establish some common ground with her pupils. This does not involve pretending that she is a teenager, or that the teenagers are older, but rather that there are concerns which all human beings hold in common. The area of death, loss and risk is definitely one of these concerns. If the teacher frankly admits that she is not in possession of the answers to questions which arise in this area, her pupils will be more likely to treat her with the sort of respect which is inspired when a teacher strikes a common chord. As we have suggested, this would involve a more relaxed interpretation of the teacher-pupil relationship, with the teacher not appearing to be the source of all knowledge. The teacher would have to be prepared to listen with respect and interest to the views of pupils, and in the area of death this can be genuinely accomplished, since in a sense the views of pupils are no worse, prima facie, than the views of their teachers. The teacher can learn a lot from pupils, and vice versa, and here we have a topic which is obviously relevant to everyone's life. Introducing more direct discussion in PSE can have the effect also of adding a sense of urgency to much of the content of the teaching programme. Much of that programme is related to the area of death, and when that relationship is made explicit pupils have a clearer view of the seriousness of the topic. They may still frustrate the teacher by appearing not to relate it to themselves in any more than a superficial manner, but the teacher will at least have given them the opportunity to run with the idea. Teachers cannot oblige pupils to take what they are told seriously. Pupils are more likely to take a topic seriously, though, if they see that their teachers are genuinely interested in their views on it and if it is a topic for which the teacher does not have a pre-conceived solution.

There is plenty of scope, therefore, within PSE for discussion of death and related issues to take place. What has to be carefully considered is the way it is done. Teachers have to be sensitive to the ways in which particular pupils may react to such a topic, and while teachers will attempt to make the issue a vivid one for their pupils, they have to be careful not to make it too vivid, for then it may both repel and attract in unhelpful ways. That is, pupils may be frightened by what they hear and see in such lessons, and as a result be unable to understand the point which the teacher is trying to make. On the other hand, they may subvert the message which the teacher is trying to get across by regarding the activity which is being described as all the more intriguing because of its connection with death, and perhaps a rather spectacular death at that. Although no doubt many PSE teachers are capable of getting the balance right, there is a lot to be said for treating death as a topic of relevance to the curriculum as a whole. This makes it possible for it to be considered in a factual and calm manner as an everyday aspect of what that curriculum describes. Teachers are also seen not to be trying to manipulate directly the feelings of their pupils when they raise the topic of death. Rather, they are using death to illustrate aspects of the curriculum, and this encourages young people to treat death as just one among many important issues which need to be considered if one is to gain an accurate understanding of that curriculum.

There will always be cases where pupils require contact with a teacher to result in that teacher listening to the pupil's problems. Sometimes pupils have problems in connection with death, risk and loss, and they find it useful to take these problems to a teacher, to a teacher they think can offer good advice with respect to the problem. As we have seen, sometimes pupils will go to teachers for support and not even mention the problem, and yet feel that they have received the support, and the resolution of the problem, which they require. One of the problems with the rapid changes in schooling over the last ten years or so is that teachers are less able to play this role than they were in the past. Teachers are far more tied up with paper work, committees and assessment than was the case in the past, and the constant changes in the structure of schooling and the curriculum have had a debilitating effect upon the ability of teachers to involve themselves in giving advice to pupils about non-academic issues. It is difficult for a pupil, especially a pupil who may lack confidence as a result of what is troubling him, to intervene in the busy day of a teacher, who is dashing about the school with a pile of papers, and ask her to help him with something personal. There is a tendency for teachers to take a rather narrow interpretation of their role and to see the emotional problems of their pupils as not something they can address. A middle-aged teacher of mathematics in London put it like this:

> When I started teaching I would spend a lot of time with pupils talking about what was bothering them, and I think this was useful. We got to know the kids quite well, and if someone started to play up, or not turn up for school, we would take them aside, sit them down over a cup of coffee and find out what was bothering them. What was good about this is that it would help our relationship, you know, the teacher-pupil relationship, and we could often nip problems in the bud. For instance, a child in one of my classes had recently lost his mother and was getting quite depressed by it all, and we had a chat, and I think I helped him to understand that we knew what he was going through, and we felt for him, and if there was anything we could do which would make life easier for him, he should tell us ... I don't think that happens so much now. I don't have the time, for one thing. I think all the government wants us to do is to test the kids, and if some of them drop through the net because they have a problem or something, well, that's too bad. We're more like technicians now, and that does not work for a lot of kids. They need more than that from their teacher.

This is far from being an unrepresentative response to the present situation in schools. Teachers feel harassed, and this is an unlikely atmosphere in which to offer to do extra work or undertake tasks which are going to be unrecognized by the school's authorities.

An additional feature of life in today's schools was mentioned by many teachers, and that is the often troubled relationship between teachers and parents. Teachers are reluctant to get involved in the private life of their pupils since there is a tendency for garbled reports to reach parents of what went on in these sessions, and, if the parents do not approve of what the teachers have done, they may well threaten to sue or at least complain to the headteacher. One teacher I spoke to had discussions with a pupil over a fairly long period of time about issues connected with sexual behaviour, during which the teacher was concerned to emphasize the importance of making sex as safe as possible. When the parents found out about these conversations, they made a huge fuss, threatening to take legal action and withdraw their daughter from the school, and they wrote a vast number of letters to the head-teacher, governors, local authority and any other body they could think of. Fortunately for the teacher concerned she had not done anything for which she could be suspended or disciplined, but it was very harrowing for her to be subjected to this sort of onslaught. Sexual behaviour is of course a very dangerous area for teachers to discuss, but it might be thought to be of vital importance, especially to older children, since it is not now just a matter of sexual ethics and the dangers of becoming pregnant or unwell. It is literally a matter of life and death, and teachers will want to ensure that their pupils are aware of the potential dangers of particular kinds of sexual activity. Yet the effects on the teacher of entering this sort of area can be severe.

Even if a teacher does and says nothing which is not sanctioned by the school, the report on what went on which is received by the parents can be garbled and inaccurate. Parents may have a rather narrower view of what schools should cover than teachers, and so are liable to complain when they discover what their children have been discussing in school. When a fuss is created, a lot of stress results for the teacher concerned. Their colleagues might not be very supportive and the school management may be annoyed that it has to get involved in what it regards as an irrelevant and awkward controversy. The inevitable conclusion which many teachers arrive at is to avoid any situation in which personal issues can arise. The motto I have often heard is 'Watch your back'. Teachers tell each other never to get involved in an unnecessary situation which can result in conflict with parents or the school authorities. They often encourage each other to stick to a narrow interpretation of their job, something which perhaps follows quite naturally from the nature of the contract which the government has imposed upon the profession. Teachers may regret this change in their role, but they will often stress the importance of sticking to a prudent course when dealing with personal issues. It is prudent not to get involved in a child's problems directly, but to pass the pupil along the line to someone else who has direct responsibility for dealing with such problems, someone like a counsellor or a psychologist. As we have seen, this may not be appropriate for the pupil. He may need to work with a teacher, someone he knows well and respects, as opposed to a stranger, but in the present atmosphere many teachers will prefer not to take the risk of coming unstuck through discussing a personal problem with a pupil and will seek to dispose of the situation totally by passing it on.

Responsibility for this sort of attitude lies in what is a fairly poor level of communication between the school and pupils' parents. We have argued that there are certain issues which people in our society find difficult to discuss, and that these to a degree centre around death, and it is hardly surprising that many parents will not have discussed these issues with their children. Not only is there something of a taboo about death in our society, but there is even more of a taboo about discussing death with children. Children are not supposed to be up to participating in such a discussion, and even quite old pupils will not have heard their parents talking directly about death. Bereaved pupils will often be ignored by adults and expected to get back to normal very quickly. There is good reason for such a policy, since adults worried that discussing an upsetting issue with children may serve to increase any anxiety which the latter may be expected to be undergoing as a result of the bereavement anyway. But when young people are bereaved and are suffering conflicting emotions as a result, when they are confused and worried about what has happened, it is important that they be presented with some account of what has happened and how they might deal with it. To ignore a topic just because it might be thought to be distressing can be a recipe for disaster, as many bereaved pupils report. A frequent point they make is that no one explained to them what was happening before the death occurred, and little effort was made to talk about it afterwards. Some children were even not taken to the funeral of their parents. It is not surprising that many of these children reported that even several years after the death they had not come to terms with it successfully, and they still thought of it as a personally very damaging experience.

In such an atmosphere schools are going to be wary before stepping in and raising topics with children which their parents are reluctant to mention. There is a lot of scope for parents subsequently to complain that the school is operating beyond its level of competence, and that it should stick to the formal curriculum. If death becomes a part of the ordinary curriculum, then children will be better able to cope with it when it happens. Even though parents may be reluctant to talk about it, if some solid analysis of death and related notions is part and parcel of everyday education, then children are better prepared to deal with the reality. The same justification might be given for sex education, of course, although at present parents have the right to withdraw their children from classes on the topic. This is hardly likely to happen where schools wish to include death in the curriculum, and it is up to the schools themselves to explain to parents precisely what they are doing and why. If they do this then there is less likelihood that parents will subject the school to complaints or that those complaints will seem well-grounded. It is not the role of the teacher to replicate in school the sorts of things which the child hears and sees at home. Children who come from racist backgrounds, for example, will be confronted in many schools with a direct attack upon such attitudes, and parents who complain will receive short shrift from the headteacher. A similar line could be taken were parents to complain about the treatment of death in the curriculum. Provided that the treatment promoted a balanced view and was sensitively presented, parents could have no grounds for objection.

There will always be a place in schools for specific teachers and areas of the teaching programme to be devoted to dealing with the personal problems of pupils. I have argued that it is not desirable for death and related issues to be excluded from the rest of the formal curriculum just because it has this personal and potentially distressing aspect. If these issues are explored by using the formal curriculum then they come to be seen as ordinary and normal topics which are capable of calm and objective treatment. Not only can these issues be dealt with academically, but they can also be used to help people make sense of the problems which arise in their personal lives. We do not then have to ask whether the role of the teacher is primarily that of a pedagogue or a social worker, because we can see that these two roles are to a degree combinable under the same label. It is not the responsibility of the teacher to sort out the personal problems of her pupils, but it is her responsibility to give those pupils the tools for the job. She should know whom to refer them to if they appear to have problems which cannot be resolved within the context of the school, but she should also know enough about problems connected with death to be able to provide some useful advice and support. I have argued that this can result in a strengthening of the teacher-pupil relationship and thus in a general improvement in the delivery of the whole curriculum. Death is too important a topic to be excluded from school, or to be enclosed within just one section of the curriculum or area of schooling. There certainly are problems to be overcome before including it, but these problems are not insuperable. Their resolution can do a lot to improve the delivery of schooling itself as well as the lives of the pupils and teachers.

Conclusion

A central problem in carrying out research on death with children is
that you speak with two groups of children who appear initially to be
quite distinct. There are children who are undergoing, or who have
undergone, a bereavement experience, and there are children who
have not. Pupils who are bereaved, and who perhaps are having problems in coming to terms with their grief, might be expected to have
different requirements of schools and teachers as compared with
children who have not been through this experience. As we have seen,
this is often the case, and schools should be appropriate places for such
bereaved children to receive support, in the same way that schools
should seek to support pupils who have other problems. Yet it is the
thesis of this book that all children in school need to do some work on
death, since death is not a phenomenon which only occurs in the lives
of some individuals. Death comes to everyone and the curriculum should
reflect this if it is going to be able to relate to real life outside school.
It may be argued that as death is surely remote from the experience of
most children, there is no necessity to include it in the schooling process
as a topic, since the curriculum cannot include everything which may
be of relevance to children. But the point I am making is that death
should be present in the thinking of all children, since they are taking
decisions which relate to death. They are taking decisions about the
sorts of things they are going to do, the kinds of activities they think
worth pursuing, and many of these projects will be based upon assessments of risk and loss. It is impossible to carry out such assessments
without considering death, and it is only when we are clear what our
attitude to death is that we can take rational decisions about our preferred activities.

The important thing to notice about death is that it plays a part in
our lives even when it is not directly apparent. Our attitudes to death
play an important role in our decisions about ourselves, and this suggests that schools have a vital role here in helping pupils to take control
of their lives. This is not a matter of telling pupils what they ought to
do, and what they ought not to do, but rather of presenting them with

an environment in which they can calmly and rationally work out what they are going to do. No doubt they will often make what their teachers regard as the wrong decision, but the important thing is that they will not have just followed a particular course of action without thinking about it. On the contrary, they will have been given the opportunity to develop their own views on their future and what risks they wish to take with the assistance of their teachers, so that whatever decisions emerge from that process are genuinely their decisions. It is something for which they must take responsibility, and they should be encouraged to reflect critically on their decisions. At the base of those decisions lies the fact of death, and it is only when we confront that fact that we can undertake the process of reflective action which is so important an aspect of our rationality. Pupils have the right to expect that teachers will work with them in acquiring the necessary skills to develop into autonomous agents.

There is no suggestion that it is necessarily easy to do this sort of thing. On the contrary, there are many pitfalls, and also plenty of advantages. We have seen how death, risk and loss are topics around which teachers and pupils can unite in their ignorance. That is, there are no experts on what our attitudes to these topics ought to be, and teachers have as much to learn from their pupils as vice versa. Teachers may well have more technical information, but certainly no moral superiority in their pursuit of answers to these difficult questions. We have here a perfect arena in which both teachers and pupils can meet and exchange views, and genuinely learn from each other. There are few contexts in education where this can really happen, and they should be encouraged. An atmosphere in which teachers and pupils feel that they can share ideas and attitudes is very positive. Effective learning and teaching is much more likely to take place in schools which occasionally enjoy such an atmosphere than otherwise.

Many children are rather critical of the counsellors with whom they have come into contact, and there is at the moment something of a backlash against counselling. There is a reason for this, in that there are undoubtedly some counsellors who adopt a rather rigid attitude to their work, only accepting as valid a narrow range of responses from children. This is a criticism which can be made of many professionals, of course, and should not be restricted to counsellors; teachers are not widely renowned for their mental flexibility when it comes to reacting to their pupils' comments and behaviour. It should be appreciated that grief counsellors are operating in difficult circumstances when they work with children because they are discussing with them a topic which at the moment is largely invisible in schools, the topic of death. Although children are naturally interested in death, it is generally ignored by schools except when it cannot be ignored owing to some major disaster or tragedy. It is unreasonable to expect outsiders to be able to enter the school, sort out the problem and then go away, and for the issue of death to disappear again until something else happens which brings it to the surface. It would be preferable for teachers and pupils to spend some time throughout schooling looking at the notion of death, and then when it arises as a personal issue for the school community it will be less shocking and inexplicable, and it will be easier to cope with. One of the pupils I interviewed suggested that it was like the fire-fighting equipment which a school uses to put out a fire having to be used all the time because the school had not taught its pupils anything about fire prevention. If pupils were more familiar with different ways of thinking about death they would find it less difficult to cope with death and bereavement when it occurs, and if the topic of death was made part of the school curriculum then it would lose much of its capacity to surprise pupils and throw them off balance.

Yet it would be far-fetched to suggest that death would lose its capacity to shock us if we spend some time thinking about it beforehand. Death is bound to be regarded as tragic in any society which deprecates loss and where religious belief is relatively weak. This does not mean that the notion of death should be ignored until it is impossible to ignore any longer, though, which is very much the strategy of most teachers and most schools. We need to devise techniques for including death in the curriculum, and although there are many claims on the curriculum from a variety of interest groups, I have argued throughout that the claims I have investigated here are very solidly grounded indeed. There are clearly cultural reasons which have led to the exclusion of death from schools, in much the same way as it has been excluded from other areas of public life, but it is not the role of schools to do no more than reflect the status quo in society. They can challenge what are taken to be the cultural norms, and often they do, when teachers invite pupils to be critical of the values of consumer culture, for example. Teachers often play down the influence which they can have on their pupils, but there is little doubt that they can have considerable influence on them, and if they use that influence to respond to the interest which their pupils have in a topic such as death, they can produce an effective and powerful environment in which a great deal of mutual learning and teaching can take place.

Advocates of curriculum change can easily fall into the trap of thinking that, if only the educational system would follow their suggestions, everything from then on will be sweetness and light. This is very far from being the case here. But there is good reason to think that the changes I am advocating could have a very positive effect upon the way schooling progresses. I have not suggested that teachers and pupils get involved in following a rigid formula for the discussion of death, since, as I have argued throughout, there is no one right way of dealing with the issue. What is important is that it be discussed, and the absence of death as an educational topic has been shown to be a potentially significant factor in retarding the emotional and academic development of children in school and beyond. Many pupils and teachers find death a very difficult topic to confront. Schools can be very unfriendly places for children with experience of bereavement, and there is dissatisfaction among many pupils and teachers with the way counselling about such problems takes place at the moment. This is an issue which needs to be addressed in school and indeed in other contexts too. Death is by no

means an easy topic to raise within school, but it can be a very rewarding area for teachers and children to explore.

Appendix 1: Methodology of the study

A purposive sample was produced, based on the variables of age, gender, ethnicity, socio-economic class, education and religion using both questionnaires and in-depth interviews. The qualitative sample cannot be random or entirely representative, but it did select types of subject relevant to the investigation. Access to the children and teachers was gained by contacting schools, and potential respondents were invited to fill in a questionnaire which provided information on their backgrounds and attitudes. They could fill it in anonymously, in which case they were not contacted further, or they could indicate that they would like to take part in an interview. Data on 750 pupils and teachers were collected through the questionnaire, and the sample was generated as a result of this information.

The main means of data collection was by interview, which was carried out in a naturalistic way with the researcher being happy to respond to issues raised by the respondents. The interviewer was of course primarily concerned to raise the issues of death, risk and loss, but discussions were often wide-ranging. The interviewer also took part in classroom activities, and spoke to a number of young people and adults outside of any educational context. Over 200 individuals were directly interviewed.

All names have been changed, and respondents were encouraged to select the name which identifies their conversation. Some respondents preferred to be labelled in terms of their gender and ethnicity, and this has been done in the interviews when requested.

Some of the respondents approached the interviewer for counselling, and arrangements were made for them to see the appropriate professionals.

Although no attempt has been made in this book to provide a complete account of the interviews along the lines of a scientific analysis of them, it is important to give more details: 223 individuals were interviewed from the school community, and 39 adults unconnected to schools were also interviewed; 100 pupils were interviewed in groups of 10, and 21 teachers in three groups of 5 and one of 6; 5 teachers and 51 children were interviewed individually; and 46 parents were interviewed individually. Of those unconnected to schools, 18 adults were interviewed together in groups of 3, and 21 were interviewed individually. The research tried to select informants who would provide a representative section of the school and adult population, but the emphasis of the study was very much on urban society, and only one rural school and community was involved in the research. There was no evidence from that particular area that the response in rural communities would be any different from that in urban and suburban environments, but this is something which requires far more study.

Some 491 lessons were observed, and data were collected by the researcher taking notes and recording conversations. A total of 43 schools were involved, and an attempt was made to use schools that gave a reasonably representative sample, as indicated by the results of the questionnaires and the breakdown of different schools and socio-economic communities in the United Kingdom. There is no suggestion that the results are representative of all British schools, only that they do give a picture of many such schools and a flavour of their attitudes to the issues under study.

When the researcher was carrying out the interviews which were recorded on tape, the informants were shown the pause button on the machine, and they were encouraged to use it to exclude from the record anything they did not want recorded. Assurances of complete anonymity were given, and no precise indication of the school's locations is provided in case this would lead to their identification. The informants were shown the transcripts of the interviews and were given an opportunity to object to the representation of their views or to the form that the lesson took. In no case did this result in a desire by either them or the researcher to change the record.

Interesting ethical issues arise when researchers raise issues that are potentially of considerable impact, especially when the informants are children, sometimes very young. One obviously requires the permission of the school before working with young children, and the school can be relied upon to have a good idea of how individual pupils will react to potentially stressful questions. It would in every case be wrong to raise with children issues that one had good reason from the beginning to expect to be upsetting. On the other hand, children can become upset during an interview; in such circumstances the researcher is obliged to bring the session to a conclusion in a manner that will end the child's distress. It has to be said that at no point during any of these interviews did this situation occur. The young people involved were happy, and indeed often eager, to discuss the issues which the interviewer introduced, and the latter often found himself trying to phrase euphemistically events which the interviewees immediately translated into blunter and more potentially upsetting language.

There are advantages to interviewing people both by themselves and in groups. In the latter case there is always the danger that they will say things to impress others in the group as opposed to expressing their real feelings. On the other hand, a group of people may stimulate each other to develop and explore ideas which they would find difficult to do by themselves, and a group interview can be a less threatening experience than the one-to-one approach. It is important that the interviewer is open to whatever the informants have to say, and does not indicate what sort of responses are expected, since children in particular are skilled, through their experiences of schooling, at picking up hints and responding appropriately. A variety of approaches is likely to be beneficial. It is also important for the interviewer to build up a good relationship with informants, and to encourage them to speak frankly, since otherwise they will be reluctant to be open about personal experiences that might be subject to public disapproval, or even legal sanction. During the interviews the interviewer did not take up an openly judgemental attitude to the activities of the informants, although clearly some of their information was deserving of moral disapproval. The interviewer told the informants that no report of what took place in these sessions would be passed onto the authorities, parents or the police, and this trust was not broken. On the other hand, when the interviews were completed the interviewer did suggest to the informants that there could well be problems with some aspects of their behaviour, and arguments were produced to show why this was so. It was up to the informants to take these remarks as they wished.

Some readers may be critical of the way in which the researcher failed to intervene during the interviews, but it was felt that this would be unhelpful for the free flow of information. It is always difficult to disengage oneself morally and emotionally from people whom one is interviewing, and indeed it is impossible to do so entirely. But it is important not to impose one's own ideas on the interviewees, and to allow them scope to express themselves in whatever way they feel is appropriate. Pupils are sophisticated devisers of the opinions and intentions of their teachers and visitors to the classroom, and it is often problematic to come out blankly with what you are actually interested in investigating. It may be better to approach the issue in a roundabout manner, by developing a conversation on an apparently unrelated topic and then gradually working towards what is of particular interest. This was the method followed in this research, and it was not difficult to carry out since the links between death, loss and risk and other areas of life are so easy to establish. Although the interviewer had a good idea of the issues which were to be raised, the ways in which they were raised and reached differed in many cases. However, for the sake of useful comparison, it was necessary to try to impose a common structure on the various encounters and discussions which ensued. This can be observed in the appendices, which give quite extended details of some of the interviews and observations, and also in the examples of conversations which appear in the text itself.

How 'scientific' are the results of this research? If by 'scientific' is meant 'universally valid', then the answer is probably that the research was not very scientific. On the other hand, it does point to some interesting observations on the issues of death, loss and risk on the part of at least some children and adults, and readers are invited to reflect upon the nature of these observations. Another researcher talking with different children and adults might come to different conclusions, and indeed a different researcher talking with the same informants might arrive at alternative observations. What we have here, though, is a slice of reality, not perhaps the only way in which reality may be sliced, but none the less a valid and accurate view of how the world seems to some people. It is hoped that these observations by children, adults and the researcher will provide a useful staging-post for future work in the area.

Appendix 2: Interviews

Key to the interviews
A = Asian
AC = Afro-Caribbean
W = White
M = Male
F = Female

AIDS, sexual behaviour and risk

There is no doubt that the onset of AIDS has changed the sexual behaviour of many people, and responses to the disease are an interesting indicator of attitudes to death. Interviews with children in the 14 to 17 age group reveal quite a diversity of views on AIDS, with class playing an important part in this diversity. Young people with a middle-class background are more likely to treat AIDS as a problem to be seriously considered. This interview with young people who came from a predominantly working-class area is quite indicative of the responses I received from many similiar communities.

Q. Do you think that people of your sort of age, your friends perhaps, are worried about AIDS?
A. No, not really. It's not really an issue for my mates. I mean, if you asked people about AIDS, they might say that it did worry them, but if you look at their behaviour, what they do like, you can tell that they don't. It's just one of those things that grown-ups go on about. (WF 1)
A. The thing is, what you've got to understand, is that we don't actually know anyone with it, or who has had it, or anything like that. Isn't it just something you get if you're gay? I remember when Mr Jones in school came in with a red ribbon on his jacket, and we asked him what it was all about, we thought then that he must be gay. He told us that several of his friends had AIDS, and we

thought he must be gay, then, and we're not gay (*lots of giggling*) so why should we bother? (ACM 2)

Q. But you don't have to be gay to catch AIDS, do you?

A. Yes, well we know that, but we don't know anyone who has caught it, and we're not gay anyway, so we're not likely to get it, are we? I mean, we *could* get it, all right, but I don't know anyone who has, so why worry about it? I mean, there are lots of worse things to worry about. (WF 1)

Q. What do you mean by 'worse things'? AIDS is something anyone can catch, surely? Don't you think it might be an idea to take precautions?

A. Yes, well it would be a good idea, I suppose. It seems very far away, though. I mean, does anyone know anyone with it? (*General shaking of heads.*) That's what I mean. We just have so many different things to think about, that's not top of the list. (ACM 3)

Q. AIDS takes a long time to develop, or can do. It may take a long time before you know that you, or your partner, are ill, and then it's too late. Doesn't this make you worry about it?

A. Yeah, well we know that, don't we. (*But it is obvious from the expressions on many of the faces that they do not.*) We've been told that. Perhaps, though, if we've got it, or are going to get it, by the time we're sick they will have discovered a cure for it, a pill or something. Anyway, they change their minds about what's good for you and what's bad for you all the time. I mean, I can see why we should be worried, but we're not really. If you start worrying about everything which can go wrong, you'd go mad, I mean, you wouldn't do anything at all. That's what they'd like, for us to stay at home all the time, like they do, and be careful about everything, and frightened. When I'm old I'll do that, but not now. (WM 3)

A. I was at a party recently, and there was this girl I met there, I know her a bit, and I thought that I'd try to get off with her. She seemed keen, and I knew from my mates that she had gone with blokes before, and we were both a bit drunk and it was obvious that we were going to do it, and I thought for a bit that this is a girl who has been with quite a few other people, and perhaps she might have picked something up from them, and I wondered if I should use anything. But she seemed keen on me anyway, and I hate condoms, so we didn't use one. It was a thought at the back of my mind, just a very quick thought, and it came and went just like that. I mean, I suppose I was a bit worried, if I used a condom, would she think that there was something wrong with me? Would she think that I thought that there was something wrong with her? What we wanted to do was to have sex, not worry about anything else. I was worried that she would not really want to have sex, I wasn't going to mention anything like AIDS to her, was I? I think that is what all my friends would have done, I mean, gone for it and worried about it afterwards, if then. (*General nods of agreement.*) (ACM 9)

Q. Does that mean that you just do not think about the risk of

AIDS, or other sexually transmitted diseases, or pregnancy, when you are about to make love to someone?

A. Well, that's not right. I do think about it, sort of briefly you wonder if this girl has had lots of boyfriends, but it's her job to sort out the pregnancy problems. It's something you think about, but not for long and not really when you are with someone new. Funnily enough, it's something you think about more when you know someone better, you sort of discuss things like pregnancy and what you are going to do about it, but it's not something you can really talk about when you first get to know someone. I mean, you spend some time trying to get off with a girl, you might have been trying for a long time, and then when everything is down for you you are not going to spoil it by asking her about AIDS; I mean, it would hardly turn her on, would it? I do wonder about it afterwards, though, and I think, well, if she went with me, perhaps she has gone with a number of blokes before me, in fact, I know she has, and I hope she has not caught anything off them and given it to me. But that's life, isn't it? You are more likely to get knocked down by a bus than to get AIDS, aren't you? I think so, anyway. If you worried about everything like that, you would never do anything at all, just stay at home and look out of the window. (WM 4)

A. I think girls worry about it more than do boys (*general nods of agreement from both boys and girls*). Especially about pregnancy. Because in the end it is down to the girl to make sure that she does not get pregnant. I know it should not be like that, but it is; after all, it is the girl who is going to get pregnant and have the problem, not the boy. The first time I had sex I did not get him to use a condom – I think I was so surprised at what happened that I don't think I had time to say it – but ever since then I wouldn't do anything like that. I mean, it has to be a condom now or I won't go any further. Mind you, I don't think much of condoms, because although I've only been with a few boys, in my experience they often break, and then where are you? I mean, you have done everything you can do to protect yourself, and even that does not work. And that means that any sort of sex is dangerous, because even kissing can be dangerous, can't it? So are we supposed to not do it at all, then? For me, it is not that sex is so wonderful, because it isn't. I mean, I could live without it as an experience. What I like is getting close to someone, getting to trust someone, because you have to trust him to treat you right, you are pretty defenceless once you are doing it, and then going on to develop a sort of relationship from there, or maybe not. But it could go in the right way, and you find out a lot about each other, and you could become a couple, and even get to live together and get married. And that's all risky. Everything's risky. There's nothing you can do about it. (WF 11)

Q. Suppose it was possible to take just one pill, with no side effects, and that pill meant that there was no possibility of getting pregnant, or AIDS, or anything you did not want to get as a result of sex. Would you take it?

A. Of course we would (*general agreement*). Then there'd be no risk. You could just relax and enjoy what you were doing, and not have to think about it. It'd be like taking drugs and not have to worry about parents, the police and getting caught, and anything bad happening to you, getting addicted, for instance. Wouldn't that be great? (WF 5)

A. But I don't know that it would be that great. Because when you come to think about it, it is the risky part of the whole thing which is part of the fun. I mean, suppose you could go up to anyone you wanted and say to her 'I want to make love to you', and she'd just do it, and there was no problem about it, couldn't be, well, it would be great for a bit but I think it would get a bit boring after a while, and what you've got to realize is that one of the things I really like about going with girls is that you never really know what's going to happen, whether they are going to go with you, and what's going to happen after it all. It could be that you'll get ill, or pregnant, or AIDS, you never know, and whatever you do it could still happen, and that's life, that's what makes life interesting and worth living. Sometimes you win and sometimes you lose. (WM 6)

A. There's something in that. Suppose every time you walked into a betting shop you won. I mean, whatever you chose, it came in first. It'd be brilliant for a bit, but then it would get boring, there'd be no fun in winning if you couldn't lose. And that's how it is with this AIDS thing, not that I really think about it, but you sort of know it's there somewhere in the background and can strike at any time, and of course you hope it will not happen to you or to anyone you know, but it could, and as it could, it makes it all more exciting, not knowing what's going to happen. It's like that with smoking. I mean, I smoke and I wonder if I'm going to be the sort of person who is going to get sick from it; I just don't know, I mean, the thought is always there in the background, but it's part of what I like about smoking, not just the taste but I'm sort of saying that I don't give a shit about the risks, if it happens it happens and I'm not going to let it ruin my life, worrying about it. Worrying's for old people. (ACM 2)

It is interesting to contrast the previous interview with similar questions put to an equally multicultural group of secondary pupils, but this time in a middle-class catchment area.

Q. Do you think that people of your age, your friends say, are worried about AIDS?

A. Yes, it's something which most people I know have thought about to some extent or other. (*Lots of nodding.*) We spend time in school discussing it, and we've got a pretty good idea how it can be acquired, through sharing needles, unprotected sex and so on. (ACM 1)

A. It's something my family goes on about a lot. They get rather boring about it, actually, but I suppose it's important and worth knowing. I mean, since there is no cure, anything which can lead to it should be avoided. (WF 2)

A. I don't know anyone with it, but that is not surprising, since it takes so long to move from being HIV [positive] to [having] AIDS. It would be stupid to ignore it just because I don't know anyone with it, that would be like thinking that one couldn't catch anything unless you knew someone with it. (WM 3)

A. It could be that by the time we're a bit older they might have discovered a cure for AIDS, and so it will not matter that much whether we catch it or not, but it is a bit of a risk, isn't it, to make your life depend upon something being discovered by scientists? I couldn't do that. (WF 4)

Q. Do you tend to take precautions when you are in a situation in which there is risk of AIDS?

A. Yes, well, I have to say that I do not spend that much of my time going out with girls, I suppose I am in most of the time working for my exams and just doing schoolwork generally. I'm not into drugs and I'm not gay, so I guess there really isn't much of a problem. I know they say that everyone is potentially at risk, but that is not really the case, because if you are careful about the things you do, and just do not do a lot of the things which are risky, you are highly unlikely to get it. I mean, you are not even that likely to get it if you don't worry about risk and just go around sleeping with whoever you like, and taking drugs and all. I mean, it is pretty hard to get AIDS. (AM 2)

A. I suppose when you think about it we are in a fairly safe group because we do not go out much, and when we do it is with people we know well and have known for a long time. There is not much opportunity for casual relationships to arise. Some of the things I see other people do are frightening. I mean, it sounds sort of romantic to meet someone at a party and then go off and perhaps make love, but to take no precautions, that's incredible. The people who are into drugs, well, they cannot be that bothered about themselves anyway, so it is a waste of time asking them to take precautions, but we don't know anyone who takes those sorts of drugs, with needles, I mean, anyway. (WM 4)

A. I remember that some time ago I went to this party, and got quite high, and there was this girl who I knew a bit, and we got sort of very friendly, and we ended up making love. It just seemed right at the time. We did not use anything – I mean, I did not think it was going to happen so I did not take anything with me – and when I thought about it afterwards I felt that I had been a complete idiot; I mean, anything could have happened as a result of that. She could have got pregnant, we could have got AIDS, I felt really guilty. Not that I forced her to do it, but it was such a stupid thing to do, really. We could have died. (WM 5)

A. The thing is, we do not on the whole go out that much, I suppose we lead pretty boring lives. Our parents have pretty strict rules about what we do and they expect us to reach certain goals, and if we do not, they nag us about it. And I suppose it is reasonable, since they want us to get to college and get jobs and that, and we

can only do that if we put in the work, and it is a bit of a waste
of time then to spend a lot of time doing the sorts of things which
other young people do, like clubbing it a lot and doing drugs. That's
not going to get you anywhere. It might be fun for a bit, but not
only might they catch something nasty, they will miss out on careers
and all that. I want to make something of my life, not catch some
fatal disease right at the start of it. (WF 3)

A. What you should realise is that we have a fairly strong idea of
where we want to get to, in career and personal terms. There is a
goal in sight, it may be distant but we know what we want to do in
the future, or at least we have some idea of what we want to do.
To get there we have to work now to pass exams and tests to get
what we want, and we have to put back the enjoying ourselves a
bit until we get there. (ACF 2)

Q. What is your attitude to risk? Do you think you share any
particular attitude to risk?

A. I think we are all different to a certain extent. I mean Jim likes
to go climbing, which I think is a bit too risky for me, and I ride
my bike without wearing a helmet, which some people think is pretty
dodgy. Everyone is different. (AF 3).

A. I suppose the only thing we have in common when it comes to
risk is that it is something we think about. I mean, even Jim
thinks about what he is doing when he is about to climb, and he
sets out to minimize the risk, to make sure it is as safe as it can,
and I think we would think someone was pretty scatty if they did
not think about the risk they were undergoing when they got
involved in anything potentially dangerous. So you wouldn't just
leap into bed with someone without taking precautions, or at least
unless you knew a lot about them. Some people would say that they
would not make love to someone, anyone at all, because it is too risky,
unless that person is your only partner (*general cries of
disagreement*). Some people would say it was OK as long as you
used precautions. Would any of us say it was all right without using
precautions? (*General shaking of heads.*) The thing is, we might
have different opinions, but I think we would take account of risk
before we acted. We don't want to act like idiots. (WM 6)

A. If you got too worried about risk, you just would not do anything
at all. You can get killed anywhere doing anything, I suppose, even
sitting at home watching your TV someone could break in and kill
you, or the roof could fall in and so on. The point is not to get so
worried that you don't do anything at all. It is worth considering
risk because that is a way of taking control of your life, of saying
who you are and what you want to be. I mean, if some lad tries to
get me to go to bed with him, well, I might, but I want to know
what precautions he is going to use. My life is valuable to me, and
I'm not going to say, 'Oh, yes, do whatever you like to me. I don't
care if I get pregnant, I don't care if I catch something from you.
Just go ahead.' There are things I want to do in the future and I don't

want everything to be mucked up by a casual sexual encounter. (WF 3)

A. My father told me that he felt a bit sorry for me growing up in a world with AIDS, because when he was young it was not a problem and the worst thing that could happen was pregnancy or the clap or something like that. But I don't think it really is worse. I mean, I don't think he would have just dived in without thinking when sex was concerned. He would have thought about it a bit, and then taken the right sort of precautions, or at least thought what those precautions might be. I mean, he is a bank manager now, and he must have been a bit of a bank manager then. I can't see him just throwing caution to the winds and getting stuck in. AIDS has not made much difference, it just means that the costs of getting it wrong are higher. (WM 1)

Young children and death

This is a transcript of a conversation between a class of 6- and 7-year-old children in Manchester with whom I had been working over a brief period. We had visited a local churchyard and had spent some time looking at the inscriptions on the gravestones.

Teacher: What do you think happens when people die?
About half the class: They go to heaven.
Teacher: Does everyone go to heaven?
John: No, only some people, good people. The others go to hell.
Teacher: Do all bad people go to hell?
Janet: Some stay in the ground, I think.
Teacher: What happens when you go to heaven?
Patricia: You go to live with Jesus, in the sky, on a cloud.
Teacher: And what do you do there?
Patricia: You look down on the world and see what goes on.
Fiona: When my nan died, everyone was crying and I said, 'Why are you crying? Isn't she going to live with Jesus?' They said that they were still sad that she was gone, but I said that it was good that she was with Jesus and that, and she could have a good time up there with him.
John: When my dog died, and I cried, my mum said that he was now in pieces [*I think he meant 'in peace'!*] and that I should not get very sad, but I was sad, and when I think about him even now, and how he'd jump on my bed in the morning, I feel I'm going to cry.
Teacher: If you just go somewhere else after your death, why do you think people get upset about it?
Monica: It's that you have no choice, you have to go away, and people who are still here miss you, and they want you to come back, but you're dead and you can't.
John: I think dead people can come back, like ghosts and things.
Teacher: Did your dog come back?

John: No, well, he's not a person, is he? But I think I can still hear him sometimes, around the house.

Monica: I don't think you can come back if you're dead. I mean, if dead people could come back the earth would be full of dead people along with the living people, and it isn't. I think that when you die you stay dead, and that's it. It's like when you have had a lolly; I mean, when you have had the last lick, that's it, there's nothing left, it's gone. It's sort of died.

Patricia: It would be nice, though, if when people died they had a sort of choice, they could come back if they wanted, and if they didn't they could stay dead. Then if people were very sad that they had died they would not have to be sad all the time, and if people were sad because someone else had died they could have them back. I mean, when we looked at the graves, some of the people were very young, and they could not have wanted to die, and their parents would have wanted them to stay alive, but some people, like very old people, I mean, they might be ill and lonely, and they might like to die.

Jack: I remember my grandfather when he was alive, he was living alone and sat in a chair a lot, but I don't think he wanted to die when he did, and we didn't either.

Teacher: Do you think that there is a right time to die?

Monica: Yes, I think that after you have been alive for a long time some things start to get a bit boring, and you are doing the same thing all the time for ages, and it could be, might be that you'd want to go away for good, and that death would be all right then, it would be something you'd want. But I don't think that children should die, because we've got lots of new things to do and that, and we're not fed up yet.

John: I think for some people, though, there is never a right time to die, 'cos they just want to go on and on, and that's all right, but you can't, and I suppose that if everything was all right you could just go on and on without having to die.

This is a conversation with a 4-year-old girl whose older sister had recently died in a road accident. The surviving sibling was having problems in adjusting to the loss.

Teacher: What do you think has happened to Veronica?

Jill: She was crossing the road, and a car came and hit her, and then she was taken to the hospital, and she died there.

Teacher: Is she going to come back?

Jill: Yes, I think so, but my mam said that she had gone to live with God, but I think that God would let her come back if she wanted to, and she does want to, because if she knew that I was playing with her toys she would want to come back and stop me.

Teacher: Have you seen her?

Jill: Yes, sometimes she talks to me and tells me things, things about school and about Tiger (*the cat*). She's dead but she's still here.

Teacher: Is that possible?

Jill: Yes, you can be dead and you can still be doing things, and you get up out of the ground and you go back to your house, but no-one can see you.

Teacher: It might be fun, if no one can see you and you can play whenever you want to and go to bed when you like, so do you think it is good to be dead?

Jill: Well, it's *quite* good, it's better not to be dead, because everyone else cries when they think about you, and that's not good, but you can still do things, but not as many things as when you're not dead.... When a man came into our school to talk about roads and crossing the road I cried when I thought of Veronica, and he asked me why I was crying, and I told him it was because my sister died crossing the road, and he cried too, and all my friends cried ... sometimes when I look out of the window at school I see Veronica standing in the corner of the playground where she used to stand and I feel very sad.

Teacher: So you think that Veronica is still with you?

Jill: Yes, she's still with me, but a bit less every day. It's like when you make a tattoo on your hand with biro, it gets weaker every day, and in the end there is nothing there, just a sort of smudge.

Teacher: Will she go away one day, then, for good?

Jill: No, she'll be with me all the time, but I won't know she's there so much.

Teacher: Does Veronica speak to you still?

Jill: Yes, she speaks to me *sometimes*, like when I'm crossing the road.

Teacher: What does she say?

Jill: 'Be careful'.

Older children and death

Older children have quite definite views on death and what it means, and are very clear on what death means to them. This conversation with teenage pupils in London brings this out.

Teacher: What do you think happens when people die?

Frank: Well, their bodies rot if they are buried, and if they are cremated they get turned into ashes, and that is the end.

Teacher: Is that generally the view? (*Nods of agreement.*) Doesn't anyone have a different view because of their religious beliefs?

Sharon: I'm a Christian, but I don't think that the Christian view is really any different. I mean, it is not the case any more that the Church preaches that if you are good you go to heaven and if you are evil you go to hell, it is far more complicated than that. It is far more complicated than that. I have a friend who is an evangelical, and he does hold such a simple belief, but I would say that it is pretty rare even among Christians. I have been to a few funerals now, and when the priest says that the body is being consigned to the ground in sure and certain knowledge of the resurrection I look

round and see if I can see any evidence of such firm belief in the
people there, and on the whole I cannot.

Ali: Yes, it's like that for Muslims too. I think most Muslims in this
country do not understand literally the parts of the Qur'an which
talk about the next life. I think most Muslims think that once you're
dead you're dead, and that's the end of it all. That is not to say that
your good deeds and bad deeds won't continue to have some effect
on the world, because they will, but the idea that some people will
wake up in paradise, while others will wake up somewhere else, no,
I don't think many people believe that any more.

Teacher: When do you think you came to have these views about
death?

Peter: I think when you are very young it is very difficult to
understand death. It is much nicer to believe in heaven and all
that, and you think of God like a father and Jesus as his son, and
when you are dead you will go to live with them. I don't think that
young children make much difference between being dead and being
alive, I mean, much distinction, because they do not have much
experience of it and they do not really understand what is going on
when people die.

Teacher: Do you think that people of your age spend enough time
talking about death?

Jasbir: I think we do, really. I mean, in school we talk quite a bit
about issues like war and euthanasia and that, and how far the
health service should go in keeping people who are going to die
anyway alive. We do talk about these things a lot.

Peter: The trouble with those sorts of topics is that they do not seem
very realistic. I mean, we are not ourselves likely to be involved in
a war or in a decision about whether to kill someone, to put someone
out of their misery, that is. These are improbable situations for us,
and I think it would be good to look at death a bit more in terms of
situations which are a bit more familiar, like drugs and smoking
and that.

George: Yes, I'd support that. It's funny, but there is not much
discussion of death in our society, it is as though it doesn't really
exist. When we talk about drugs and that, it is always about how it
is illegal or unhealthy, but not really about the fact that these
activities, well, they are going to kill you, or they could kill you.
After all, that is what is ultimately wrong with certain kinds of
behaviour, they will kill you if you carry on with them, and I think
that this should be emphasized, I mean, people don't want to die.
When you do something dodgy I think it is there in the back of your
mind that this is dangerous, this could kill me, and I think it ought
to be brought out to the front of your mind, 'cos that's where it
belongs.

Jean: There's something in that. I mean, what I hate about all this
stuff about sex education is that it is so trivial, it's all about not
getting pregnant, and not getting AIDS, but the thing is, the
important thing is, staying alive. I mean, it is not much fun getting

pregnant, right, if you don't want to, but what you should do is say to kids, 'Right, you can get pregnant, but most important, you can get dead,' and that would have an effect. That would really frighten them, they'd listen then. But you can see that the teachers don't want to talk about that, it's a bit heavy for them, they just want to go on about being pregnant and that, but that's not that important, staying alive is.

Hayden: I agree with that. There would be no point in going around telling kids that they had to worry about getting killed, because, well, really, at our age we're not that bothered about it. I mean, we know that AIDS is a pretty remote possibility unless you're gay and a drug user and that, and there isn't much point in getting us to worry about something which doesn't worry us, if you see what I mean. But what they should do is try to get people of our age to think about what they're doing, because what they're doing can get you killed. I suppose we're more likely to die of smoking than of anything else, especially the girls, and I think they ought to lay it on the line, that if you want to smoke, OK, but this is what is going to happen. It's not that it will make you unattractive, that lads will not fancy you because of your breath and that, although that might be true, but it's going to kill you, and there's nothing more important than that.

Sharon: The thing is, you can tell that the teachers think we're not up to thinking about that, they think the only things which are important to us are our looks, our relationships with boys, but that's not true. Some things are more important than that, like staying in one piece. I don't think the teachers should go around, like with a bell shouting, 'You're going to die,' but they should say that some ways of acting are likely to end in an earlier death than would happen otherwise, and they should stress this, because it would have an effect. That should be the main point, and the stuff about looks and so on should come later.

Jasbir: What the teachers do is, they look at the stuff we read and what we say and do, and they say, 'Oh, these people are only interested in clothes and raves and that. They're not up to thinking or talking about anything else.' But it's not true. We do like to have a good time, but that is not all we think about. We do think about other things, we worry about the future, and if they were going to treat us with respect they'd talk about other things, more important things, like what can happen to you if you smoke and drink and do drugs and that. We'd be more responsible if they treated us [as] capable of acting more responsibly; well, some of us would, anyway. Let's talk about how people should behave, how even teachers should behave, what risks we should take, how we should behave when things go wrong, and let's work out what our attitudes are going to be to these sorts of issues, what it's like to have no money or job, and let's get our ideas sorted.

Reacting to disasters

When a disaster hits a school, there is a tendency nowadays for it to be visited by counsellors, who are there until the immediate trauma is resolved, and who may visit subsequently when children and teachers exhibit signs of anxiety as a result of the tragedy. Some teachers refer to the arrival of the counsellors as 'another disaster', while others think that they are useful and have a valuable role to play in such situations. It is difficult to know how one could evaluate the role of counselling in such circumstances. From the interviews I have conducted opinions among teachers and pupils are fairly evenly divided, and I have included a report on this conversation because it seems to me to be quite representative of many similar conversations. It would be invidious to provide details which would be sufficient to identify the school, and so all the reader needs to know is that the school was shocked by a major road accident killing and injuring quite a large number of pupils. The school is a secondary institution in a large city.

Interviewer: What happened after the accident?
Bill: We had an assembly, at which lots of the pupils were crying, and the head told us about the accident, and he said that we should carry on as normal, but that there would be lots of counsellors coming to the school to discuss the accident with us, and that we should talk to them about what we were feeling.
Interviewer: And how did that go?
Celia: Well, I did not like it, because I thought, and a lot of us thought, that we did not want a load of strangers coming into the school, people who did not know us and who we did not know, especially just then, when we were all upset, and we had the feeling that what they were doing, well, it's their job, isn't it, they didn't really care. At a time like that you just want to be by yourself, with your friends I mean, not with a load of new people.
George: What was quite useful was that they told us that we would be having lots of confused feelings about what had happened, and I suppose that had a point to it, but I think we could have worked that out for ourselves, and it was not as though we did not have anyone to talk to about it, because we were all talking about it, with our friends and teachers, with people who knew the children who'd died, not with strangers. I mean, I suppose if there was no one to talk to, it would have been better to talk to a stranger than to no one, but there were lots of people to talk to; we are in school, after all.
Celia: What annoyed me about the counsellor I talked to is that she seemed to want me to say certain things, that I was having certain sorts of feelings, and it did not take me long to work out that she expected me to have those feelings, and there were some feelings which I ought to have and some which I shouldn't have, and it's like with the teachers sometimes, you make out that you agree with them because it's simpler to do that, it saves time and trouble. I mean,

she was nice and I didn't mind talking to her, but I would have preferred not to, just to talk to my friends and that. I think at a time like that you don't want to have to deal with new people, with strangers.

Alison (a teacher): I thought the counsellors did a good job. The children were all very upset, as were the teachers; I did not know what to say to them, and it was good to have someone there who did. I felt entirely lost during the whole episode, even though I knew the children well, and I had no idea what to say, or how to get back to normal. I mean, how do you get back to normal in such a situation? The counsellors explained to us what feelings we might be having and how the children might react, and that was a help. We did get almost back to normal after a few days. . . . I wish I could have known what to do myself, because I felt that the children were looking to me for a lead, and I just could not provide one. The counsellors could do something, at least.

Margaret: I would have liked to talk to the teachers more, and not with the counsellors. Of course, the teachers were crying and that too, but I think we could have talked about it, no problem. They did after all know the kids who were killed, and it's better to talk to someone who knows them, knew them, than a stranger.

John (a teacher): It is about a year now since the accident, and it is certainly not forgotten. We are reminded of it whenever there is a similar accident, and the children and the teachers relive their experiences and feelings from before. I think the children look to us then to do something, but I don't think we really know what we're supposed to do. We refer any pupil who appears to be especially upset to a counsellor, and there have been some children who found it very difficult to come to terms with the accident, even now. I think the accident did draw us all closer together, but I am not sure that we are dealing with it appropriately. I don't think we know what to do.

Interviewer: What do you think schools should do about accidents like that?

Sean: I think that we should sort of prepare for them, because people get killed all the time, I mean, it is not as though it is a great surprise that there are crashes on the road and people die, or that people die in different circumstances. I remember in my previous school we had a chemistry teacher who was dead keen on fire drill, and he was forever practising with us what we would do if there was a fire. I mean, he got us to imagine what it would be like for there to be a fire, and we had to go out, not panic, and he would go for the extinguisher, and he showed us how it worked and that. One day there was a fire, there was a bit of a bang in the chimney which took away the fumes and the plastic melted and there were all these flames everywhere. We were not bothered, we had prepared for it, and we walked out calmly with him, and he went right back and put it out. I mean, we knew that there would be a horrible smell and smoke and that, and we did not panic, we

knew what to expect. I think if we hadn't prepared for it, it would
have been really bad, we'd have been really scared and upset about
it. He even managed to turn what had happened into a chemistry
lesson, and we had to work out how it had happened, what the
chemical changes were in the things that got burnt. It should be
like that with accidents and when pupils get killed. We should
be prepared for it, 'cos it happens all the time. That doesn't mean
that it wouldn't be very sad, because it would. But we would know
what was going on, we would discuss it, and I think the right
people to talk to are ourselves and the teachers. I mean, we all know
the people who died.

Audrey: I agree with that. I mean, these counsellors, they're nice,
don't get me wrong, but it's just their job, isn't it? They didn't know
the kids who were killed or hurt. They come here because they got
paid to come. I suppose that is true for the teachers too, but at
least they knew the kids. I remember when my dad died this
undertaker came to the house and he told me that he was very
sorry for my loss, but he wasn't really; I mean, if my dad had not
died he would not make the money he made out of the funeral. I
mean, he did not even know him. Just because we're not old it
doesn't mean we're idiots. We knew that the counsellors were trying
to help, that it's their job to help, but we'd have preferred them
not to have come, and for us to have been able to just talk among
ourselves.

John (a teacher): The good thing about the counsellors is that they
gave us, the teachers, some idea about what to do and say. I think
they were more important for us than for the children. I thought
Sean made an interesting point in his fire-fighting analogy, and I
suppose we ought to prepare children more for emergencies and
disasters and so on, but I don't know how we could do so. There is so
much we already have to do, and to take on this as well, it wouldn't
be easy. I am a person with twenty years' teaching experience and
I had no idea what to do then, and really I have no idea what I
should do in the future.

Alison (a teacher): I know it is a terrible thing to say, but the
accident did bring us together, not just the pupils and the teachers,
but the teachers themselves. The antagonisms which had built up
in the staffroom just vanished, for a bit, and we all felt much more
of a team. It did not last for very long, and I think that was a shame,
because I think that if we were more of a team more of the time,
we would cope better with disasters like that. I mean, children would
be more prepared to talk with us about their problems, and we as
teachers could be more open about our feelings. We should not really
need outsiders to come in and tell us about how we should feel
after an accident or what we should do with the kids, we should
know this ourselves because we are prepared to discuss those feelings
openly. The counsellors can do this, because they are not part of the
discipline thing, but I think we could maintain discipline and also
have an atmosphere in which we could talk to each other about what

we are feeling. It's just that there are some things which never seem to arise for discussion in school, and death is one of them, which is a real problem when something happens which makes it important to discuss.

Appendix 3: A guide to the literature

There is a wide variety of material on the topics of death, loss and risk, but there is not much which relates these topics to schools in perceptive and useful ways. The academic analysis of death and related issues often seems far removed from a practical understanding of how they might be utilized in the classroom or in more individual conversations with children. Although I have argued throughout that these issues are central to the educational process, they are not normally regarded as such and teachers tend to avoid them. Yet the research which does exist on death can throw an interesting light on practical issues in schooling, and it is worth examining the broad outlines of the academic discussion in order to place the argument of this book within a broader theoretical perspective. This will provide readers concerned with education with a grasp of some of the wider issues relating to their work.

Until quite recently, it was widely accepted that the Western world is a predominantly death-denying society. Ariès (1962, 1974, 1981), Becker (1973) and Gorer (1965) argue that we do all in our power to deny death and ignore its inevitability, while Illich (1977) and Kübler-Ross (1970, 1975, 1989) discuss the medicalization of death, the way in which we have tried to confine it within the technical environment of the institution, specifically the hospital. When people are about to die, they are removed from the home and the family and attended by professionals, and after death the body is disposed of through the services of other professionals, the funeral profession. This is often taken to be in marked contrast with the Middle Ages, when death was more of a family affair in which relatives and friends would participate, and when even the young would gain a familiarity with death. Now death is far more invisible. People are more likely to die in hospitals, hospices and other institutions than at home. Few if any of the dead person's associates are likely to be present at the bedside. We have become progressively more socially distanced from death, and this has led to the popular observation that death has replaced sex as a social taboo. It is not a topic which one expects people to discuss to any great extent, and even thinking about death can be labelled as 'morbid', especially in the young.

This approach has been thoroughly criticized by Walter (1989, 1990,

1992), who argues that we should beware of providing over-simple explanations for complex social phenomena. There is evidence of a reluctance to think and talk about death in our society, but he also points to evidence that there is often a lot of interest in death, and suggests (Walter, 1989) that death is hidden rather than forbidden as a topic. This is very much in line with the argument of this book, and Walter's article can be taken to be a useful corrective to the slogan that death is a taboo. What needs to be done to explore the 'death as taboo' thesis is an investigation of the ways in which the media represent death, and the ways in which those representations are read by different sections of the audience. We also need to carry out far more research into the ways people talk informally about death, and how the social, ethnic and gender divisions of the population vary in their response to death. Little of this work has so far been done and apart from a few case studies, there is no general account of how reactions to death are affected by social differentiation.

Psychologists have argued that there are distinct stages in the feelings of those who have suffered the death of someone to whom they are close, or who are terminally ill. In some highly influential research, Bowlby (1980) examined the implications of the attachment between mother and child. He found that there is a strong yearning that children experience when separated from their mothers. He argued that this urge to search for a loved one from whom we have been separated is an instinctive reaction which can be observed in acute grief. Bowlby outlines four phases of mourning which he thinks occur generally in detachment or loss. They normally follow this order:

1. Numbing – which can last from a few hours to weeks and which is followed by intense distress and anger in short bursts.
2. Yearning and searching for the lost person, lasting months or even years.
3. Disorganization and despair.
4. Reorganization, which can take a variety of forms.

Kübler-Ross (1970) argued that many dying people initially refuse to accept what is happening to them, and try to deny that they are dying. This is often taken to be a consequence of the notion that death is a taboo and so we have to try to distance ourselves from it. Once the denial phase is over and the dying person begins to appreciate that she is really dying, she often gets angry and/or depressed. Death cannot be avoided, though, and most dying people come to terms with this fact, thus moving to the acceptance stage. Although there is a temptation to see these stages as being universal, they probably are not, and there is scope for individual differences in behaviour, although Parkes has argued that there is broad agreement that mourning and bereavement follow a specific course with identifiable elements

There is clearly an important connection between bereavement and stress. The death of a loved one is often given as the main cause of stress, and an unsatisfactory coping with a bereavement has been described by Dora Black (1987) as an important cause of future depression and mental illness. Grieving and mourning had a significant place in earlier times, and both the grievers and those around them knew what was expected of them in terms of social behaviour. Gorer argues that these practices gave support to the bereaved and helped others to know how they were to react to them, since there were public indications of their status as mourners. Today the only rituals associated with death and bereavement in Western society are quite subdued, and neither the bereaved nor their friends have a clear idea how they are to behave. If this leads to the repressing of emotions then this could cause trouble at a later date, since grief needs to be worked through. Unresolved grief can persist with a person for many years and eventually become pathological, resulting in some form of mental illness. In the absence of socially effective grieving mechanisms, there is a need for bereavement counselling to provide the appropriate therapy which will prevent these problems from arising. Although much of the research which has taken place has concentrated on death, it is often just as relevant to loss, and indeed for some people a type of loss which does not involve death will be more potentially stressful and harmful than one which does involve death. People may be expected to react to loss in similar ways to the description of reactions to death.

There is an extensive literature which looks at the ways in which the health status of individuals, their access to health care and the quality of provision of that care are influenced by their social and occupational class, gender, ethnicity and geographical location. It has been known for a long time that class influences mortality rates to a marked degree (Townsend et al., 1992). There are differences in the mortality rates of infants depending upon the country of birth of the mother. As far as gender is concerned, life expectancy estimates in 1988 show that on average new-born girls could expect to live six years longer than new-born boys, and there are higher levels of male deaths in all age groups than female deaths. There are also considerable differences between males and females in terms of actual causes of death. For example, in 1985, in the 1 to 14 age group, 40 per cent of deaths among boys were due to accident and violence compared with 26 per cent in girls (DHSS, 1986). Although class and gender are important factors in influencing death, occupation is also significant, as is geographical location (Aggleton, 1990). There is no doubt when one looks at the statistics dealing with morbidity that death and illness occur at different stages in the lives of the population, and in different forms. Adolescents are more likely to indulge in risky behaviour and to die violently. To be poor, to belong to an ethnic minority which originates in the developing world, to live in particular parts of Britain, all constitute disadvantage as far as morbidity is concerned. Although death is universal, it comes to us in different ways depending upon who we are and where we live, and these differences obviously affect the experience and understanding of death of particular individuals.

There has been an enormous amount of literature which looks at how schools work, how pupils relate to teachers and what shape Personal and Social Education should take. The issue of how far the curriculum should be integrated, which was a popular concern in the 1970s, is no longer directly raised in the same form, but it does emerge powerfully in the extensive discussions which have taken place over the past twenty years or so over the direction of the school curriculum. The frequent changes in government policy with respect to the curriculum, and the constant tinkering about with it which has been such a familiar feature of recent education policy, have returned the curriculum to the top of the list of topics to be discussed, and not only by those who are specialists in education. The rapid changes in the system of schooling, which have often led to considerable increases in stress among teachers, have obliged teachers to think carefully about the nature of their professional role. The increasing prospect of redundancy owing to lack of finance for the educational system, the introduction of performance-related pay, the competition of schools for pupils and the reliance on a narrow level of educational aims as a criterion of teaching success are likely to change the nature of the occupation. Many of these changes will not be in the direction which we have advocated in the discussion of how schooling might be improved. On the other hand, moral panics over teenage sub-cultures, drugs, health, AIDS and moral education are likely to increase interest in many of the points which have been made here.

Most of the work which has been developed on death and education has been carried out in the United States, with a certain amount of interest in the topic as a mainstream subject in Israel also. Most of the courses in the United States take place within higher education institutions, but there are also a large number of different courses on death and dying in high schools. The content of such courses varies a great deal, but they tend to share some common features. These are:

> Historical and cultural background
> Thoughts and feelings about death
> Death, loss, separation and grief as related ideas
> Dying
> Bereavement
> Suicide
> Death education
> Counselling issues
> Consumer issues

Americans see death as an important aspect of the curriculum. Public schools in the United States are secular, and so they need to deliver ideas about life and death through the ordinary curriculum. They cannot expect these ideas to be transmitted through religious observances in the school. Also, many American schools view suicide as a serious problem, and they wish to discuss with their pupils the nature of this action, to prepare them better to deal with their personal problems in less dramatic and final ways.

The consumer aspects of the course often take the form of advising pupils how not to be cheated by the funeral director! One of the intriguing features of many of the courses in the United States is their combination of the practical and the spiritual. This can make for a very effective combination, since there is likely to be something there which will be of interest to everyone in the class. American children seem to be far more prepared to discuss their feelings and emotions with each other and with their teachers than are British children, and although readers will find much of interest in the American literature on death and education, it could not be used in a British context without a great deal of transformation.

The courses which are used in Israel tend to put the emphasis upon counselling. Since Israel as a state has been perpetually at war for a very long period, most Israeli children are surrounded by images of death and have personal experience of some sort of bereavement, teachers feel it is important to be aware of the problems which pupils may be having and how to resolve those problems. When teachers are trained in Israel they are formally prepared to participate in the adjustment of pupils to the experience of grief and bereavement. Schools are well prepared for problems which individual pupils may have, and are often prepared to discuss those problems openly with the whole class, although not of course referring directly to particular pupils. Pupils are even open to issues such as appropriate mourning behaviour, or how far the religious understanding of death and suffering can be accepted. For example, Sephardi Jews (those originating in the Middle East) have far more demonstrative mourning rituals than do Ashkenazi Jews (those originating in Europe), and these groups will often argue with each other in school over which rituals are most appropriate. The Sephardim argue that their rituals make it easier for the bereaved person to adjust to normality, while the Ashkenazim regard very dramatic grief behaviour as bad taste and unacceptable. These sorts of debate are useful for the child growing up in Israeli society since they help him or her to think about the implications of death and how they are going to prepare for it.

The closest we approach to such a context in this country is in the schools of Northern Ireland, which are often in communities which have been seriously affected by death and loss. One might expect that in Northern Ireland there would be an approach similar to that in Israel, or at the very least like the American system of dealing with death and dying. Yet there is no such intervention in the curriculum, and the only changes which have been made to schooling to reflect local conditions have been done on an *ad hoc* basis. There is nothing strange about this, since it should be recalled that the majority of schools in the province are denominational, and so there is scope for issues connected to death to be dealt with within the context of a religious approach. The various communities in Northern Ireland are stable and have been drawn even closer together by the prevalent violence, and there are acceptable ritualized ways in which grief and bereavement may be expressed. Finally, the situation in Northern Ireland is more like a disaster affecting a whole community rather than a series of arbitrary tragic events, and, as we have seen, this provides a far more supportive environment in which bereavement can take place.

The important lesson to be derived from looking briefly at the variety of approaches which have been undertaken in different contexts is that there is no blueprint for success which can be expected to work everywhere and at all times. This is an important consideration to bear in mind when looking at the books which are available for children in school and which discuss death and loss. We have to bear this in mind also when we look at the materials which have been prepared for teachers. It would be invidious to seek to evaluate these teaching resources, since some teachers will find them effective for the context within which they are working, while others will not. Individual teachers will wish to stress particular points, and they will find some books more appropriate for this than others. Death and grief are such complicated phenomena that it is impossible to have books for children which will encompass all aspects of such issues in just one book. It is useful for teachers to have a check-list of themes in mind when assessing books for children, and some of the themes which one would expect to find are as follows, in a list adapted from Greenall (1988):

> Expressing anger
> Behaving out of character
> Coming to terms with the reality of what happened
> Reactions of others
> Fear of others dying
> Significance of funeral or cremation
> Need to say goodbye
> Expressing sadness
> Long-term consequences

It is fair to say that a good deal of literature for secondary-age children deals to some degree with death, risk and loss, and teachers will not find it difficult to find appropriate material for this age group. This is especially true when we look at what is known as 'teenage' literature, which reflects some of the more serious aspects of teenage psychology. There is an extensive treatment of these issues in both fictional and non-fictional literature. We have suggested that teachers are not on the whole very willing to use this literature to help develop classroom discussion on the topic of death.

For children who are younger than secondary level, there is also a wide variety of literature, and some of the books for very young children combine excellent graphics with clear and sensitive text. If one is working with a child whose parent is dying, or who has a potentially life-threatening disease, there are particular points which one wishes to get over to the child. These points are potentially emotionally charged and the teacher should be prepared to take them up with the child. If this happens, then the child will benefit from clear messages which will help reduce his guilt after the parent or close relative dies and which will support the person who will subsequently be responsible for the child's care. These messages are:

> One day the main carer will no longer be around.
> The child is not to blame.

The carer will not return.

It is important to share feelings while the carer is still alive.

It is necessary to prepare for difficult times ahead.

The child should acknowledge the existence of both pleasant and unhappy events in his life with the carer.

The carer has spiritual and religious beliefs which may support the child after death.

Death may have terminated the caring relationship, but not the love of the carer for the child.

Someone will care for the child after the previous carer's death.

One of the ironies of the thesis that death is a taboo in our culture is that books on death and how to prepare for it are so ubiquitous. There is a rich variety of literature at every level, some of which is very good, and much of it is highly appropriate for use with children in school. All that is required is for teachers to be prepared to use it.

Bibliography

Guide to the bibliography

The bibliography is indicative only, and is designed to alert the reader to some of the main texts on the subject of death. For ease of access these have been subdivided under several headings followed by an alphabetical list. Many of the books listed provide information concerning yet more works on the topic.

Before the bibliography proper, there follows a separate list of references cited in the text.

References

Aggleton, P. (1990) *Health*. London: Routledge.

Ariès, P. (1962) *Centuries of Childhood*. London: Cape.

Ariès, P. (1974) *Western Attitudes to Death: From the Middle Ages to the Present*. Baltimore: Johns Hopkins University Press.

Ariès, P. (1981) *The Hour of Our Death*. London: Allen Lane.

Becker, E. (1973) *The Denial of Death*. New York: Free Press.

Black, D. (1987) Depression in children. *British Medical Journal*, **294**, 462–3.

Bowlby, J. (1980) *Attachment and Loss*, Vol. 3: *Loss, Sadness and Depression*. London: Hogarth.

Department of Health and Social Security (DHSS) (1986) *On the State of the Public Health 1985*. London: HMSO.

Gorer, G. (1965) *Death, Grief and Mourning in Contemporary Britain*. London: Cresset.

Greenall, B. (1988) Books for bereaved children. *Health Libraries Review*, **5**, 1–6.

Illich, I. (1977) *Limits to Medicine: Medical Nemesis*. Harmondsworth: Penguin.

Kübler-Ross, E. (1970) *On Death and Dying*. London: Tavistock.

Kübler-Ross, E. (1975) *Death: The Final Stage of Growth*. Englewood Cliffs, NJ: Prentice-Hall.

Kübler-Ross, E. (1989) *Living with Grief.* London: Sheldon Press.
Marcuse, H. (1966) *Eros and Civilization.* Boston: Beacon.
Peters, R. (1973) *Authority, Responsibility and Education.* London:
  Allen & Unwin.
Tolstoy, L. (1960) *The Death of Ivan Ilych and Other Stories.* New York:
  New American Library (first published 1884).
Townsend, P., Davidson, N. and Whitehead, M. (eds) (1992) *Inequalities
  in Health: The Black Report and the Health Divide.*
  Harmondsworth: Penguin.
Walter, T. (1989) Secular funerals. *Theology,* **92,** 394–402.

Childhood, death and society

Two very important collections of readings are:

Dickenson, D. and Johnson, M. (eds) (1993) *Death, Dying and Bereave-
  ment.* London: Sage.
Papadatou, D. and Papadatos, C. (eds) (1991) *Children and Death.* New
  York: Hemisphere.

For work on children dying the following book is outstanding:

Hindmarch, C. (1994) *On the Death of a Child.* Oxford: Radcliffe Medical
  Press.

Hendriks, J., Black, D. and Kaplan, T. (1993) *When Father Kills Mother.*
  London: Routledge.

Anthony, E. and Kohnpernik, C. (eds) (1973) *The Child in His Family:
  The Impact of Disease and Death.* New York: Wiley.
Ariès, P. (1962) *Centuries of Childhood.* London: Cape.
Ariès, P. (1974) *Western Attitudes to Death: From the Middle Ages to
  the Present.* Baltimore: Johns Hopkins University Press.
Ariès, P. (1981) *The Hour of Our Death.* London: Allen Lane.
Becker, E. (1973) *The Denial of Death.* New York: Free Press.
Black, D. (1987) Depression in children. *British Medical Journal,* **294,**
  462–3.
Black, D. and Urbanowicz, M. (1987) Family intervention with
  bereaved children. *Journal of Child Psychology and Psychiatry,*
  28(3), 467–76.
Bowker, J. (1991) *The Meanings of Death.* Cambridge: Cambridge
  University Press.
Bowlby, J. (1980) *Attachment and Loss,* Vol. 3: *Loss, Sadness and
  Depression.* London: Hogarth.
Buckman, R. (1988) *I Don't Know What to Say: How to Help Someone
  Who Is Dying.* Basingstoke: Papermac.
Curl, J. (1993) *A Celebration of Death.* Batsford: London.
Dershimer, R. (1990) *Counselling the Bereaved.* Oxford: Pergamon.
Dinnage, R. (1990) *The Ruffian on the Stair: Reflections on Death.*
  London: Viking.

Gorer, G. (1965) *Death, Grief and Mourning in Contemporary Britain*. London: Cresset.

Hinton, J. (1972) *Dying*. London: Penguin.

Houlbrooke, R. (ed.) (1989) *Death, Ritual and Bereavement*. London: Routledge.

Illich, I. (1977) *Limits to Medicine: Medical Nemesis*. Harmondsworth: Penguin.

Judd, D. (1989) *Give Sorrow Words: Working with a Dying Child*. London: Free Association.

Jupp, P. (1990) *From Dust to Ashes: The Replacement of Burial by Cremation in England 1840–1967*. London: The Congregational Memorial Hall Trust.

Kamerman, J. (1988) *Death in the Midst of Life*. Englewood Cliffs, NJ: Prentice-Hall.

Kane, B. (1979) Children's concepts of death. *Journal of Genetic Psychology*, **134**, 141–53.

Kearl, M. (1989) *Endings: A Sociology of Death and Dying*. Oxford: Oxford University Press.

Kübler-Ross, E. (1970) *On Death and Dying*. London: Tavistock.

Kübler-Ross, E. (1975) *Death: The Final Stage of Growth*. Englewood Cliffs, NJ: Prentice Hall.

Kübler-Ross, E. (1989) *Living with Death and Dying*. New York: Macmillan.

Lake, T. (1984) *Living with Grief*. London: Sheldon Press.

Leik, N. and Davidson-Neilsen, M. (1992) *Healing Pain: Attachment, Loss and Grief Therapy*. London: Routledge.

Lendrum, S. and Syme, G. (1992) *Gift of Tears: A Practical Approach to Loss and Bereavement Counselling*. London: Routledge.

Littlewood, J. (1992) *Aspects of Grief: Bereavement in Adult Life*. London: Routledge.

Llewellyn, N. (1991) *The Art of Death*. London: Reaktion Books.

Neuberger, J. (1987) *Caring for Dying People of Different Faiths*. London: Lisa Sainsbury.

Nuland, S. (1994) *How We Die*. London: Chatto & Windus.

Parkes, C. and Weiss, R. (1983) *Recovery from Bereavement*. New York: Basic Books.

Parkes, C. (1986) *Bereavement: Studies of Grief in Adult Life*. Harmondsworth: Penguin.

Prickett, J. (ed.) (1980) *Death in Living Faiths*. London: Lutterworth.

Raphael, B. (1984) *The Anatomy of Bereavement*. London: Hutchinson.

Rosenheim, E. and Reicher, R. (1990) Informing children about a parent's terminal illness. *Journal of Child Psychology and Psychiatry and Allied Disciplines*, **26**(6), 995–8.

Sherr, L. (ed.) (1989) *Death, Dying and Bereavement*. Oxford: Blackwell.

Stroebe, M., Stroebe, W. and Hanson, R. (1993) *Handbook of Bereavement: Theory, Research and Intervention*. Cambridge: Cambridge University Press.

Walter, T. (1989) Secular funerals. *Theology*, **92**, 394–402.

Walter, T. (1990) *Funerals*. London: Hodder.
Walter, T. (1992) Modern death: taboo or not taboo. *Sociology*, **25**(2) 293–310.

Health and morbidity

A key work is: Townsend, P., Davidson, N. and Whitehead, M. (eds) (1992) *Inequalities in Health: The Black Report and the Health Divide*. Harmondsworth: Penguin.
Aggleton, P. (1990) *Health*. London: Routledge.
Department of Health and Social Security (DHSS) (1986) *On the State of the Public Health 1985*. London: HMSO.
Doyal, L. (1981) *The Political Economy of Health*. London: Pluto.
Goldthorpe, J. (1980) *Social Mobility and Class Structure in Modern Britain*. Oxford: Clarendon Press.
Graham, H. (1984) *Women, Health and the Family*. Brighton: Harvester Press.
OPCS (1992) 1990 *Mortality Statistics: Perinatal and Infant: Sociological and Biological Factors, England and Wales*, Series DH3, No. 24. London: HMSO.

Learning and schooling

Abercrombie, M. (1989) *The Anatomy of Judgement*. London: Free Association Books.
Ball, S. (1990) *Policies and Policy Making in Education*. London: Routledge.
Baum, W. (ed.) (1988) *The Religious Dimension of Education in a Catholic School*. London: Catholic Truth Society.
Carr, W. and Kemmis, S. (1986) *Becoming Critical: Education, Knowledge and Action Research*. London: Falmer Press.
Elliott, J. (1991) *Action Research for Educational Change*. Buckingham: Open University Press.
Hargreaves, A. and Woods, P. (eds) (1984) *Classrooms and Staffrooms*. Buckingham: Open University Press.
Hargreaves, A. and Fullan, M. (eds) (1992) *Understanding Teacher Development*. London: Cassell.
Holt, J. (1987) *How Children Fail*. Harmondsworth: Penguin.
Hopkins, D. (1985) *A Teacher's Guide to Classroom Research*. Buckingham: Open University Press.
Lipsitz, J. (1984) *Successful Schools for Young Adolescents*. London: Transaction Books.
Lyotard, J. (1994) *The Postmodern Condition: A Report on Knowledge*. Minneapolis: University of Minneapolis Press.
Marcuse, H. (1966) *Eros and Civilization*. Boston: Beacon.
Nias, J. (1989) *Primary Teachers Talking*. London: Routledge.
Nias, J. (ed.) (1993) *The Human Nature of Learning: Selections from*

the Work of M. L. J. Abercrombie. Buckingham: Open University Press.

Pollard, A. (1985) *The Social World of the Primary School*. Eastbourne: Holt, Rinehart & Winston.

Rattansi, A. and Reeder, D. (1992) *Rethinking Radical Education*. London: Lawrence & Wishart.

Schön, D. (1983) *The Reflective Practitioner*. London: Temple Smith.

Tizard, B. and Hughes, M. (1984) *Young Children Learning*. London: Fontana.

Williams, R. (1989) *The Politics of Modernism*. London: Verso.

Children, death and education

Of great importance for teachers are:

Ward, B. (1993) *Healing Grief*. London: Vermilion.

Ward, B. and Houghton, J. (1992) *Good Grief*, Vols 1 and 2. Available from 19 Bawtree Road, Uxbridge, Middlesex UB8 1PT.

Anthony, S. (1973) *The Discovery of Death in Childhood and After*. Harmondsworth: Penguin.

Baxter, G., Bennett, L. and Stuart, W. (1989) *Adolescents and Death: Bereavement Support Groups for Secondary School Students*. Ontario: Canadian Centre for Death Education and Bereavement.

Bernstein, J. (1977) *Loss and How to Cope with It*. New York: Seabury.

Bluebond-Langner, M. (1978) *The Private Worlds of Dying Children*. Princeton, NJ: Princeton University Press.

Blume, D. *et al.* (1986) Challenger 10 and our school children: reflections on the catastrophe. *Death Studies*, **10**, 95–118.

Corr, C. (1978) A model syllabus for death and dying courses. *Death Education*, **1**, 433–57.

Corr, C. (1980) Workshops on children and death. *Essence*, **4**, 5–18.

Corr, C. and McNeil, J. (eds) (1986) *Adolescence and Death*. New York: Springer.

Feifel, H. (ed.) (1959) *The Meaning of Death*. New York: McGraw-Hill.

Feifel, H. (ed.) (1977) *New Meanings of Death*. New York: McGraw-Hill.

Furman, E. (1974) *A Child's Parent Dies*. New Haven, Conn.: Yale University Press.

Furman, E. (1978) Helping children cope with death. *Young Children*, **34**, 25–32.

Gordon, A. and Klass, D. (1979) *They Need to Know: How to Teach Children about Death*. Englewood Cliffs, NJ: Prentice-Hall.

Grollman, E. (ed.) (1967) *Explaining Death to Children*. Boston: Beacon.

Grollman, E. (ed.) (1974) *Concerning Death: A Practical Guide for the Living*. Boston: Beacon.

Grollman, E. (1976) *Talking about Death: A Dialogue between Parent and Child*. Boston: Beacon.

Horn, S. (1989) *Coping with Bereavement: Coming to Terms with a Sense of Loss*. London: Thorsons.

Jackson, E. (1965) *Telling a Child about Death*. New York: Hawthorn.

Kavanaugh, R. (1972) *Facing Death*. New York: Nash.

Knott, J. *et al.* (1982) *Thanatopics: A Manual of Structured Learning Experiences for Death Education*. Kingston, RI: SLE Publications.

Krementz, J. (1983) *How It Feels When a Parent Dies*. London: Gollancz.

Lifton, R. (1979) *The Broken Connection: On Death and the Continuity of Life*. New York: Simon & Schuster.

Lonetto, R. (1980) *Children's Conceptions of Death*. New York: Springer.

Maurer, A. (1964) Adolescent attitudes toward death. *Journal of Genetic Psychology*, **105**, 75–90.

Pacholski, R. and Corr, C. (eds) (1981) *New Directions in Death Education and Counselling: Enhancing the Quality of Life in the Nuclear Age*. Arlington, Va.: Forum for Death Education and Counseling.

Pacholski, R. and Corr, C. (eds) (1982) *Priorities in Death Education and Counseling*. Arlington, Va.: Forum for Death Education and Counseling.

Plant, M. and Plant, M. (1992) *Risk-Takers*. London: Routledge.

Raab, R. (1989) *Coping with Death*. New York: Rosen.

Raphael, B. (1990) *The Anatomy of Bereavement: A Handbook for the Caring Professions*. London: Unwin Hyman.

Rosenthal, N. (1978) Teaching educators to deal with death. *Death Education*, **2**(3), 293–306.

Rudolph, M. (1978) *Should the Children Know? Encounters with Death in the Lives of Children*. New York: Shocken.

Sahler, O. (ed.) (1978) *The Child and Death*. St Louis, Mo.: Mosby.

Siegel, B. (1986) Helping children cope with death. *Research Record*, **3**(2), 53–62.

Ulin, R. (1977) *Death and Dying Education*. Washington, DC: National Education Association.

Wass, H. (ed.) (1979) *Dying: Facing the Facts*. Washington, DC: Hemisphere.

Wass, H. and Corr, C. (eds) (1984) *Childhood and Death*. Washington, DC: Hemisphere.

Wass, H. *et al.* (1990) Death education and grief/suicide intervention in the public schools. *Death Studies*, **14**, 253–68.

Wells, R. (1989) *Helping Children Cope with Grief: Facing a Death in the Family*. London: Sheldon Press.

Wolf, A. (1973) *Helping Your Child to Understand Death*. New York: Child Study Press.

Wynne Jones, P. (1985) *Children, Death and Bereavement*. London: Scripture Union.

General

Kübler-Ross, E. (1987) *AIDS: The Ultimate Challenge.* New York:
  Macmillan.
Shibles, W. (1974) *Death: An Interdisciplinary Analysis.* Whitewater,
  Wis.: The Language Press.
Spinoza, B. (1987) *Ethics,* in *The Collected Works of Spinoza.* Princeton,
  NJ: Princeton University Press.
Tolstoy, L. (1960) *The Death of Ivan Ilych and Other Stories.* New York:
  New American Library (first published 1884).

Bibliographical resources

A great deal of useful bibliographical material will be found in the
references already provided, but it is worth having a short list of works
which specifically deal with bibliography.

Completely indispensable to anyone interested in the area is:

Mathias, B. and Spiers, D. (eds) (1993) *A Handbook on Death and
Bereavement.* National Library for the Handicapped Child.

This publication not only provides references for 113 recent publications,
but also briefly describes each entry and classifies them in terms of the
appropriate age for readership.

Bernstein, J. (1977) *Books to Help Children Cope with Separation and
  Loss.* New York: Bowker.
Greenall, B. (1988) Books for bereaved children. *Health Libraries
  Review,* **5,** 1–6.
Simpson, M. (1987) *Dying, Death and Grief: A Critical Bibliography.*
  Philadelphia: University of Pennsylvania Press.
Wass, H. and Corr, C. (1984) *Helping Children Cope with Death:
  Guidelines and Resources.* Washington, DC: Hemisphere.
Wass, H. *et al.* (eds) (1980) *Death Education: An Annotated Resource
  Guide.* Washington, DC: Hemisphere.

Video packs

*'I Wish I Could Have Told You So': A Video Assisted Bereavement Coun-
selling Training Pack.* Christine Kalus, University of Portsmouth Enterprise Ltd, 1994.

Living with Loss. Church Pastoral Aid Society, 1993.

Of great value to anyone concerned with children, death and education
is the Open University Study Pack K260 *Death and Dying.* Although
this is not specifically directed at the area discussed in this book, it
does provide a comprehensive account of dying, death and bereavement.
The emphasis is on the health and social services, but much of it can
be adapted to schools.

Journals

A variety of journals carry articles on schools and death, but in Britain this is a largely ignored topic. The American journals

> *Death Studies*
> *Omega: Journal of Death and Dying*
> *Death Education*

deal with the issue thoroughly, but largely from an American perspective. Many of the articles tend to be quantitative in nature. There is much available in these journals which is of value to the situation in Britain, although British readers should be careful not to generalize from research carried out within a very different context.

Useful organizations

There exist a number of organizations which can be very helpful for teachers and others trying to construct a course, or parts of a course which deals with children and death. Some place more emphasis on counselling children and teachers who have come into contact with children with particular problems, and others will provide information and appropriate literature for course design. They will often be able to put enquirers in touch with local contacts who can prove helpful.

ACT
Institute for Child Health, Royal Hospital for Sick Children, St Michael's Hill, Bristol BS2 8BJ. Tel: (0117 9) 221556. Helps families whose children have life-threatening and terminal conditions.

BACUP
121–123 Charterhouse Street, London EC1M 6AA. Tel: 0171–608 1661. Provides information on cancer and on caring for patients with cancer.

BEREAVED PARENTS HELPLINE
6 Cannons Gate, Harlow, Essex. Tel: (01279) 412745.

BRITANNIA SHIPPING COMPANY FOR BURIAL AT SEA
Britannia House, Newton Poppleford, Sidmouth, Devon EX10 0EF.

BRITISH ASSOCIATION FOR COUNSELLING
37a Sheep Street, Rugby, Warks. CV21 3BX. Tel: (01788) 578328. Provides general information about advice, support and counselling.

BRITISH HUMANIST ASSOCIATION
47 Theobalds Road, London WC1X 8ST. Tel: 0171–430 0908. Provides information about secular services.

CANCER RELIEF MACMILLAN FUND
Anchor House, 15–19 Britten Street, London SW3 3TZ. Tel: 0171–351 7811.
For advice on home and hospice care.

CANCER AND LEUKAEMIA IN CHILDHOOD TRUST (CLIC)
CLIC House, 11–12 Freemantle Square, Cotham, Bristol, Avon BS6 5TL. Tel: (0117 9) 244333.
For support and information for sufferers and their families.

THE COMPASSIONATE FRIENDS
Mrs Anne Pocock, 6 Denmark Street, Bristol BS1 5DQ. Tel: (0117 9) 292778
An international organization of beareaved parents offering friendship and support – local groups in some areas.

COT DEATH RESEARCH AND SUPPORT GROUP FOR BEREAVED PARENTS
8a Alexandra Parade, Weston-super-Mare, Avon BS23 1TQ. Tel: (01836) 219010, (01934) 413333
Gives counselling and counselling training.

THE CREMATION SOCIETY OF GREAT BRITAIN
Brecon House, Albion Place, Maidstone, Kent ME14 5DZ. Tel: (01622) 688292.
Provides information about all aspects of cremation.

CRUSE
Cruse House, 126 Sheen Road, Richmond, Surrey TW9 1UR. Tel: 0181–940 4818.
Provides support and help for all bereaved persons, especially siblings.

DEPARTMENT OF SOCIAL SECURITY
Leaflets Unit, PO Box 21, Stanmore, Middlesex HA7 1AY.
Provides various guides.

FOUNDATION FOR THE STUDY OF INFANT DEATHS
15 Belgrave Square, London SW1X 8PS.
Offers support and help to parents whose children have died from cot deaths.

HOSPICE INFORMATION SERVICE (see St Christopher's Hospice entry.)

JEWISH BEREAVEMENT COUNSELLING SERVICE
Mrs June Epstein, Co-ordinator, 1 Cyprus Gardens, London N3 1SP. Tel: 0181–349 0839 (answering machine), 0171–387 4300 ext. 227 (office hours only).
Covers the London area only.

LONDON BEREAVEMENT PROJECTS CO-ORDINATING GROUP
68 Chalton Street, London NW1 1JR. Tel: 0171–388 0241.

NATIONAL ASSOCIATION OF BEREAVEMENT SERVICES
20 Norton Folgate, Bishopsgate, London E1 6DB. Tel: 0171–247 1080
Umbrella organisation for all bereavement organizations.

NATURAL DEATH CENTRE
20 Heber Road, London NW2 6AA. Tel: 0181–208 2853.
Provide advice and information on alternative means of disposal.

Worth reading in this context are:
Bradfield, J. (1994) *Green Burial: The DIY Guide to Law and Practice*,
available from the Centre.
Albery, N., Elliot, G. and Elliot J. (eds) (1993) *The Natural Death
Handbook*. London: Virgin.

PARENTS OF MURDERED CHILDREN SUPPORT GROUP
10 Eastern Avenue, Prittewell, Southend, Essex SS2 5QU. Tel: (01702)
68510.
An organization linked to Compassionate Friends.

ST CHRISTOPHER'S HOSPICE
Halley Stewart Library, 51–59 Lawrie Park Road, Sydenham, London
SE26 6DZ. Tel: 0181–778 9252.
The library contains a specialized, multidisciplinary collection of liter-
ature on care of the terminally ill, and bereavement.

SAMARITANS
Head Office, 10 The Grove, Slough, Berkshire SL1 1QP. Tel: (01753)
532713.

SANDS
28 Portland Place, London W1N 4DE. Tel: 0171–436 5881
Stillbirth and neonatal death. There are self-help groups nation-wide.

THE SOCIETY FOR COMPANION ANIMAL STUDIES
1A Hilton Road, Milngavie, Glasgow G62 7DN. Tel: (01891) 615285.
Offers a befriending service by telephone to bereaved pet owners.

TERRENCE HIGGINS TRUST
52–54 Grays Inn Road, London WC1X 8JU. Tel 0171–831 0330
For all information on caring for people with AIDS.

TWINS BEREAVEMENT SUPPORT GROUP
Mrs S. Payne, 59 Sunnyside, Worksop, Notts S81 7LN.
Gives support to families who have lost a twin or twins.

YAD B YAD (HAND IN HAND)
8 Grove Avenue, London N10 2AR.
A resource centre for parents and teachers for use mainly by the Jewish community.

Index

Given their ubiquity in the text, there are no references in the index to the terms children, death, education, learning, pupils, schools, society, teachers and young people. The only authors listed are those mentioned in the discussion of the research itself. There is a detailed list of other relevant authors in the Bibliography.

NATIONAL UNIVERSITY LIBRARY SAN DIEGO